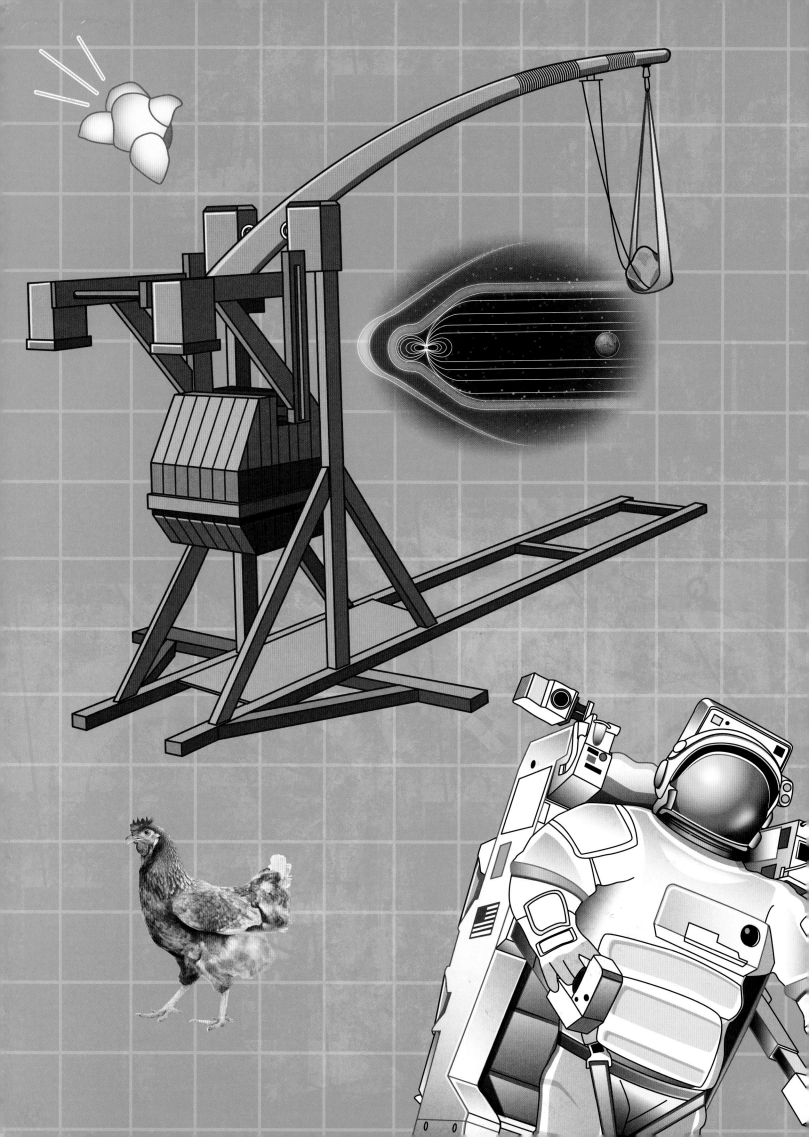

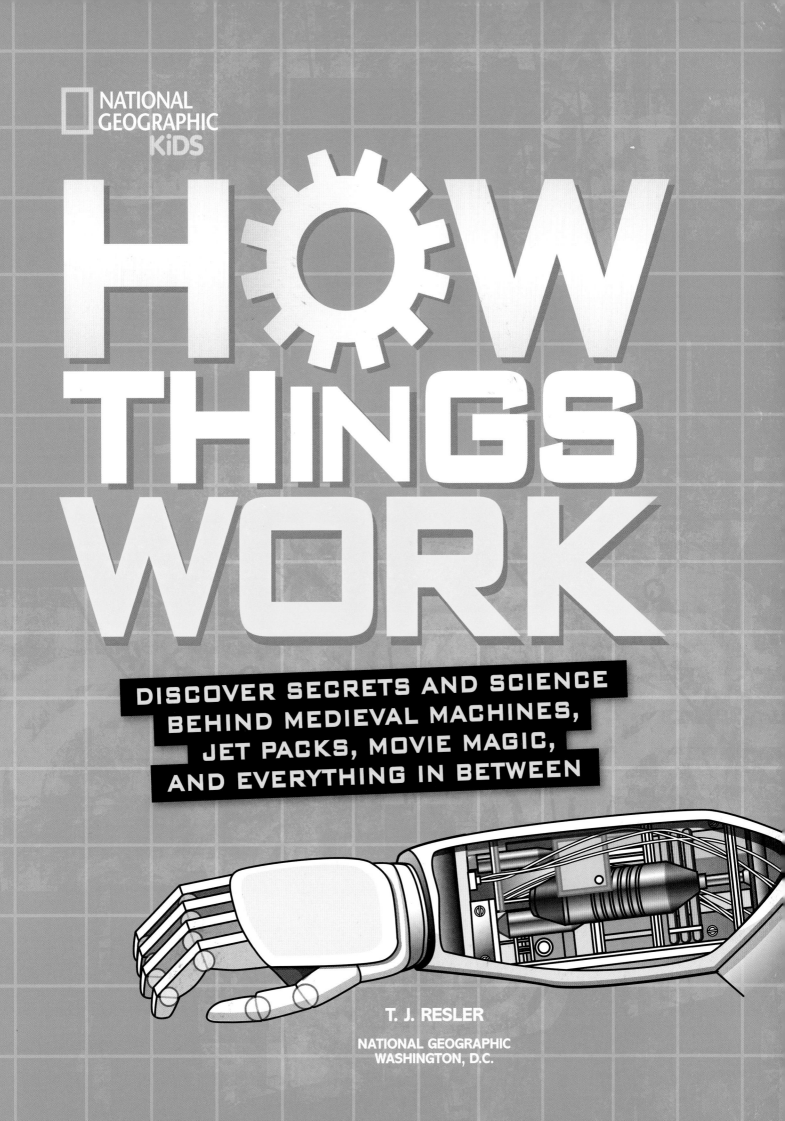

NATIONAL GEOGRAPHIC KiDS

HOW THINGS WORK

DISCOVER SECRETS AND SCIENCE BEHIND MEDIEVAL MACHINES, JET PACKS, MOVIE MAGIC, AND EVERYTHING IN BETWEEN

T. J. RESLER

NATIONAL GEOGRAPHIC
WASHINGTON, D.C.

HERE'S THE THING:

YOU'VE GOT TO BE A CERTAIN KIND OF KID TO GET INTO THIS BOOK.

YOU HAVE TO BE AN EXPLORER.

You know the type—kids who crave adventure, kids who want to find the coolest things in our world and maybe other worlds, too. Kids whose curiosity keeps growing. They want to know what's out there, why something happens, and how things work.

Are you one of those? Because, we're going to be 100 percent honest with you, this book is not for kids who like boredom.

THIS BOOK IS FOR KIDS WHO WANT THEIR MINDS BLOWN.

Even if they're chilling. Yeah, it's for kids who like to kick back, too. You know, read a book, watch a great movie, munch on some popcorn. Definitely. Oh, and about that popcorn? Maybe we should mention that this book is also for kids who like to eat. That's right, eat.

If you're one of those kinds of kids—the adventurous, kicking-back, eating types—read on. We've got you covered.

YOU'LL EXPLORE FROM THE DEPTHS OF THE OCEAN TO THE FAR REACHES OF SPACE,

and you'll learn about the coolest inventions ever—past, present, and future. You'll discover bizarre features of our Earth that rival the amazing discoveries of space. You'll whet your appetite for foods that transform into your favorite snacks. And you'll go behind the scenes to find out about the magic of moviemaking. You'll get the basics on the "Just the Facts" pages. And if you want to go deeper, jump into the "Tell Me More!" sections.

Along the way, you'll meet explorers who dive into underwater caves, discover glowing sea creatures, and reveal the mysteries of space. You'll learn about scientists who make chocolate better (what?!) and stunt performers who thrill us in our favorite movies. And, in "Tales From the Lab," you'll find out the amazing stories behind the discovery of a 2,000-year-old computer, the search for life on other planets, the creation of a whole new kind of fruit, the daring first flight into a hurricane, and the acting and animation that brings incredible creatures to life on the big screen. Whew.

But you're not done. There are a bunch of challenges to solve, experiments to perform, and creations to make. Look for the "Try This!" features and you'll be on the way. We know you're up for them. Because, you know,

YOU'RE ONE OF THOSE KINDS OF KIDS.

WHAT'S INSIDE

CHAPTER 1

BLAST FROM THE PAST

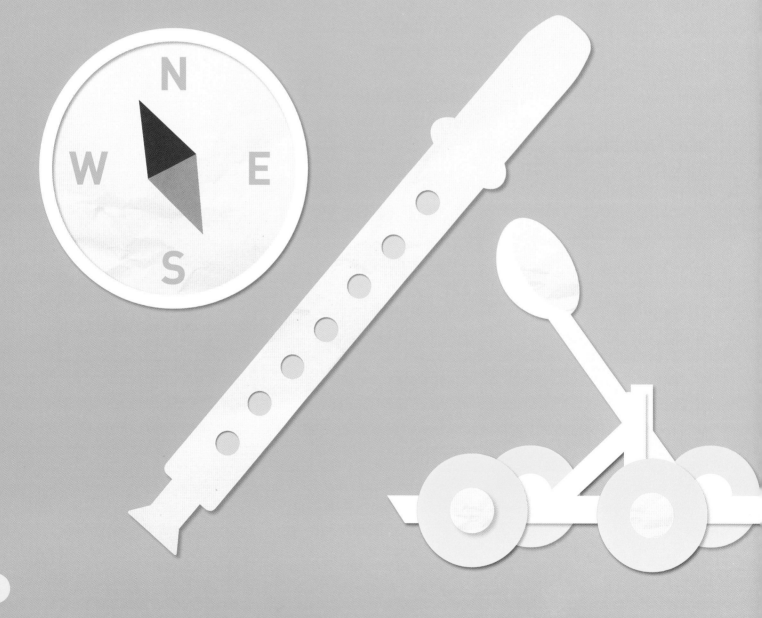

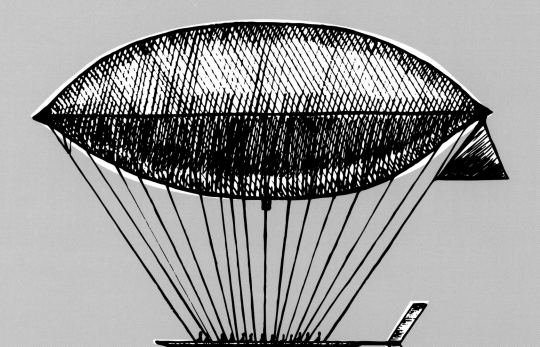

CUTTING-EDGE INVENTIONS.

Sophisticated technology. Mind-blowing feats of science and engineering. We must be talking about the latest and greatest innovations of the year, right? Not even close. Try the past, hundreds and thousands of years ago. We're going to time travel—back to times of castles and catapults, early humans discovering music, machines that sparked information revolutions and took us on our first flights. Times when ancient artisans created devices so complex that some of us thought aliens brought them from space. Oh, yeah. You'll get a blast from this past.

STORMING THE CASTLE

How did a TREBUCHET defeat a castle's defenses?

In the Middle Ages, kings and lords built ever stronger castles to keep their enemies away. From simple wooden forts in the fifth century, castles grew to massive stone fortresses by the 15th century. Protected by armed soldiers and high defense walls, they were hard to attack. Unless you had a trebuchet, a machine that hurled stones or other missiles at—or over—the walls. Hold on to your helmet, because we're checking them out.

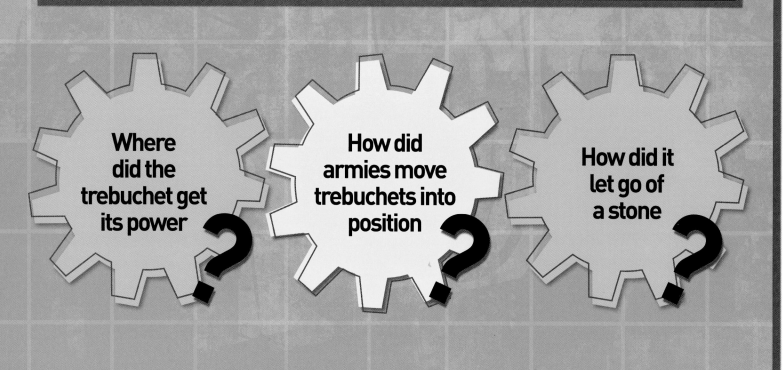

Where did the trebuchet get its power?

How did armies move trebuchets into position?

How did it let go of a stone?

JUST THE FACTS

A Smashing Success

The trebuchet, a fearsome medieval catapult, flung stones or other objects (called "missiles") at castles. It was a type of siege engine, a contraption designed to break down or get past castle walls. Though trebuchets needed to be built expertly so they'd hit their targets, their basic design was actually pretty simple. All trebuchets consisted of a lever and sling. When the lever rotated, the sling flung the missile through the air to smash the castle wall.

A traction trebuchet was smaller, but more easily moved. It could fling stones 100 to more than 300 feet (30 to 91 m).

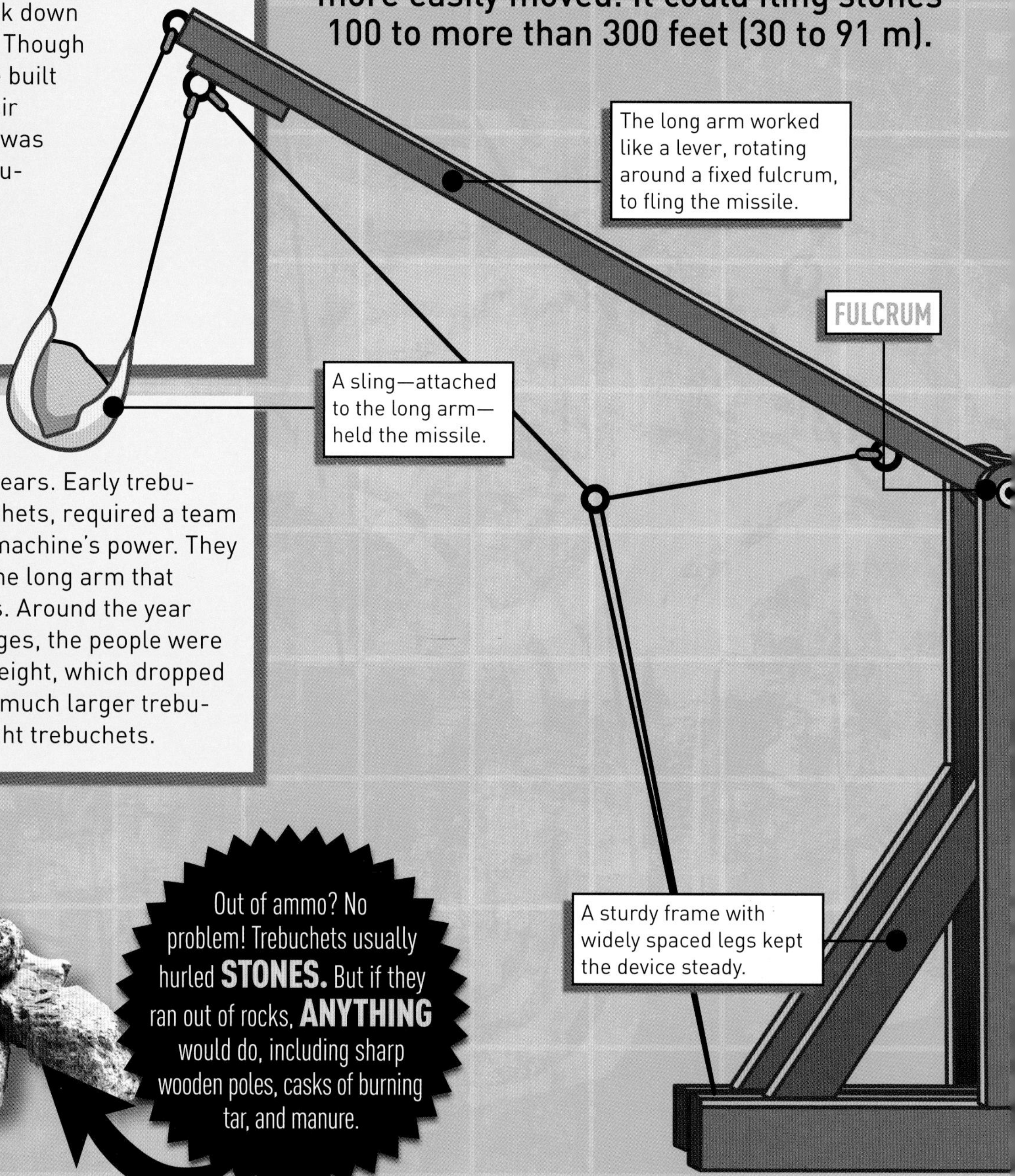

The long arm worked like a lever, rotating around a fixed fulcrum, to fling the missile.

FULCRUM

A sling—attached to the long arm— held the missile.

Weighty Subject

Trebuchets changed over the years. Early trebuchets, called traction trebuchets, required a team of people to provide the machine's power. They yanked ropes to swing the long arm that threw the stone missiles. Around the year 500, during the Middle Ages, the people were replaced with a massive weight, which dropped to swing the arm. These later, much larger trebuchets were called counterweight trebuchets.

A sturdy frame with widely spaced legs kept the device steady.

Out of ammo? No problem! Trebuchets usually hurled **STONES.** But if they ran out of rocks, **ANYTHING** would do, including sharp wooden poles, casks of burning tar, and manure.

FUN FACT —————————————

SOME MEDIEVAL EUROPEAN TREBUCHETS HAD NICKNAMES, INCLUDING "EARTHQUAKE'S DAUGHTER," "BIG MOTHER," AND "BAD NEIGHBOR."

GRAVITY-ASSISTED

A counterweight trebuchet was so large, it usually needed to be built right on site. The largest ones could fling missiles as heavy as 220 pounds (100 kg) up to 900 feet (274 m), though 100 to 200 pounds (45 to 90 kg) was more typical.

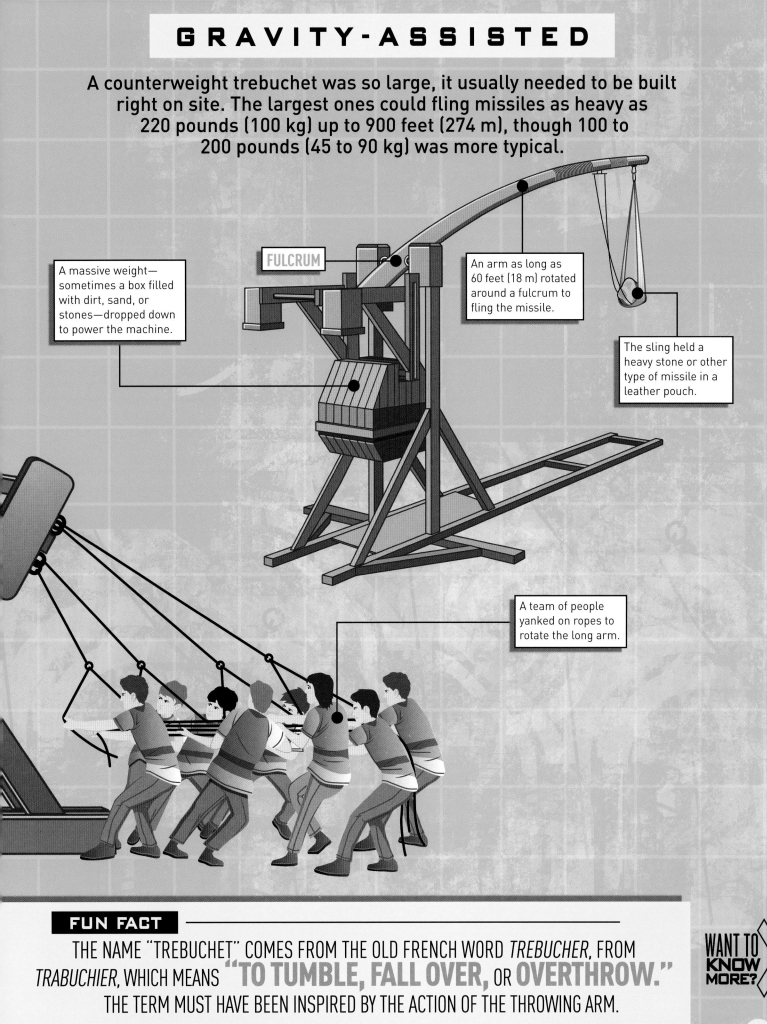

FULCRUM

A massive weight—sometimes a box filled with dirt, sand, or stones—dropped down to power the machine.

An arm as long as 60 feet (18 m) rotated around a fulcrum to fling the missile.

The sling held a heavy stone or other type of missile in a leather pouch.

A team of people yanked on ropes to rotate the long arm.

WANT TO KNOW MORE?

FUN FACT

THE NAME "TREBUCHET" COMES FROM THE OLD FRENCH WORD *TREBUCHER*, FROM *TRABUCHIER*, WHICH MEANS **"TO TUMBLE, FALL OVER, OR OVERTHROW."** THE TERM MUST HAVE BEEN INSPIRED BY THE ACTION OF THE THROWING ARM.

TELL ME MORE

SIMPLE DESTRUCTION

The counterweight trebuchet works its destruction by harnessing the power of physics. It combines various simple machines to become a compound machine. The arm is a lever with the sling at its long end and a weight at the short end. Before it's fired, the weight stores potential energy. When the arm is released, gravity pulls the weight down and the potential energy is converted to kinetic energy, the energy of motion. As the weight drops, the arm swings around the fulcrum, speeding up as it swings—a change called rotational acceleration. The throwing end of the arm is several times longer than the weighted end, so the tip of it has a longer distance to travel around its arc; it must move faster than the weighted end. The sling, attached to the arm's long end, transfers the forces to the missile, which shoots toward the target. Powerful science.

FUN FACTS

● Some **U.S. universities**—including Wright State, the South Dakota School of Mines and Technology, Weber State, and, appropriately, the U.S. Military Academy at West Point—have had students **design and test trebuchets** to learn mechanical engineering design and physics. And, yes, **they get to fire them.**

How Things Worked

When you think of trebuchets in battle, do you picture them attacking medieval European castles? There's a good reason for that. The trebuchet probably reached its height in popularity around the 12th and 13th centuries in Europe. It then continued to be used there for another two centuries! But that wasn't the beginning of its story. To find its origins, we need to turn back the clock and point our compasses to China. The first trebuchets, traction types operated by soldiers, were invented by the Chinese before the fourth century B.C. The Chinese had different sizes depending on their needs. On the small end, a quick-firing model required only two soldiers to operate. At the other extreme was the "whirlwind," a massive machine that required 250 soldiers to fire. It could launch a 140-pound (64-kg) stone a distance of more than 80 yards (73 m). The Chinese continued to utilize these siege engines for centuries, eventually developing a counterweight version, and even put some on warships. Soon, word of these marvelous machines spread. By the sixth century, armies around the Mediterranean and the Middle East were using traction trebuchets, sometimes called "city takers." They eventually added weights to the human-powered machines, creating a sort of hybrid. But it was the Europeans of the 11th through 13th centuries who changed the design all the way to a counterweight variety. For many years, trebuchets ruled the battlefield. But as cannons became more common, especially in the 13th to 14th centuries, they put trebuchets out of business.

MISSILE LAUNCHER

Every motion of the counterweight trebuchet works to accelerate the missile toward its target.

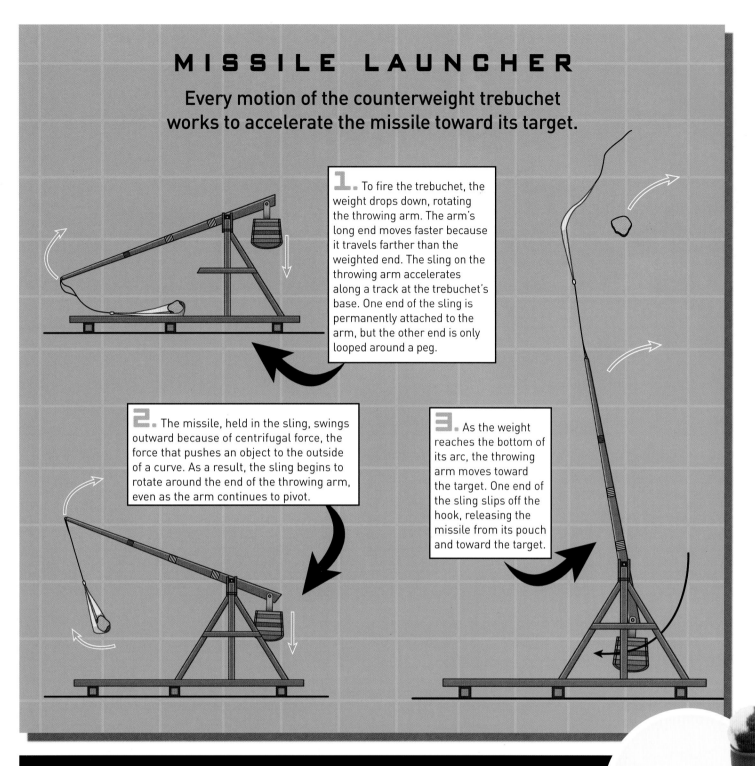

1. To fire the trebuchet, the weight drops down, rotating the throwing arm. The arm's long end moves faster because it travels farther than the weighted end. The sling on the throwing arm accelerates along a track at the trebuchet's base. One end of the sling is permanently attached to the arm, but the other end is only looped around a peg.

2. The missile, held in the sling, swings outward because of centrifugal force, the force that pushes an object to the outside of a curve. As a result, the sling begins to rotate around the end of the throwing arm, even as the arm continues to pivot.

3. As the weight reaches the bottom of its arc, the throwing arm moves toward the target. One end of the sling slips off the hook, releasing the missile from its pouch and toward the target.

TRY THIS!

No, we don't want you to storm a castle or fling deadly missiles at your little sibling. But we couldn't deprive you of the awesomeness of having your own trebuchet! OK, this isn't quite a real trebuchet—especially with its craft sticks, rubber bands, and diminutive size—but it's a real catapult. And it's plenty awesome. All you need are a few supplies: eight regular craft sticks, two jumbo craft sticks, three rubber bands, heavy-duty tape (like duct or masking tape), and some mini marshmallows or little pom-poms. Take the stack of regular craft sticks and hold them together tightly with rubber bands on each end. Push one of the jumbo craft sticks between the top two stacked sticks, so it makes a "t." Place the other jumbo stick under the entire stack, right below the first jumbo stick. Hold one end of the two jumbo sticks together with a rubber band, and tape it on top so the rubber band won't slip off. Scoot the taped end of the jumbo sticks closer to the stack, and you have a catapult. Use it to launch your mini marshmallows or pom-poms.

ANCIENT COMPUTER: DISCOVERING THE ANTIKYTHERA MECHANISM'S SECRETS

In 1900, near the tiny Greek island of Antikythera, a group of sponge divers discovered a shipwreck. The huge vessel, a victim of a ferocious storm, had crashed into the island's craggy coastline, broken apart, and sunk 160 feet (50 m) to the seabed. It lay there forgotten for 2,000 years.

The ship carried prized artworks of ancient Greece: larger-than-life sculptures of bronze and marble, ornate glass vases and bowls, and brilliant gold jewelry. Nestled among those treasures was something odd: a shoebox-size hunk of corroded bronze.

It turned out to be the greatest wonder of all.

But in 1901, when divers discovered the bronze lump, no one realized what they'd found. It would take a century—and teams of researchers—to figure out what it was: a 2,200-year-old device so sophisticated that it's been called the world's first computer.

> ## 66 NO ONE HAD SUSPECTED THEY HAD SUCH COMPLEX TECHNOLOGY. 99

A CRACK IN THE CASE

In the months following the discovery, divers worked to recover the artifacts from the deep. The treasures were whisked away to the National Archaeological Museum in Athens. At first the lump of corroded, green bronze didn't attract much attention. Museum curators labeled it "Item 15087" and set it aside.

The fragile artifact soon broke into several chunks, revealing a tiny metal gear.

A Greek archaeologist concluded that the artifact was a clockwork device related to astronomy. But how could that be? Nothing that complex existed until Europeans began making clocks in the 14th century— at least that's what scholars thought.

Archaeologists yearned to learn more, but the device's paper-thin metal parts, originally housed inside a wooden box, were held together only by hardened sediment. The artifact was too fragile to handle.

SNEAKING A PEEK INSIDE

In the 1950s, scientist Derek de Solla Price became intrigued by the Antikythera Mechanism. He studied photographs of it and, in the 1970s, x-rayed it. He traced its gears and began to figure out how they worked. He made an astounding discovery. The mechanism wasn't just a tool to study astronomy. It was a computer that showed how the universe worked.

The ancient Greeks were known to be amazing astronomers for their time, but no one had suspected they had such complex technology.

Other researchers built on Price's work. In the 2000s, an international team of experts, the Antikythera Mechanism Research Project, realized that improved x-ray and digital imaging technology could reveal even more details of the device's internal workings and inscriptions.

The team asked imaging pioneers to help. Hewlett-Packard used a photographic technique to bring the device's inscriptions into focus, and an engineer at X-Tek Systems built a scanner powerful enough to penetrate the calcified lump of bronze. The scanner, brought from England to Greece, was as big as a van and weighed more than an adult African elephant. It took three forklifts to get it into place.

But it was all worth it. "When we saw the first image ... it was absolutely amazing," researcher Tony Freeth said. "It was like a new world really."

REVEALING THE MYSTERIES

The experts discovered that the Antikythera Mechanism did far more than Derek Price ever knew.

With the turn of a simple hand crank, the device moved multiple dials and pointers on the front and back of its outer case. They showed the movements of the moon and planets, the passage of time, and the occurrences of eclipses. And they predicted each occurrence for decades. Additional dials counted the days—using at least three different calendars from ancient times— while others showed the zodiac, weather predictions, and which Olympic games would be played in a given year.

The ingenious design still amazes scientists today.

ANCIENT GREEKS BELIEVED SOLAR ECLIPSES WERE **BAD OMENS,** SIGNALING AN UPCOMING FAMINE, A LOST BATTLE, OR **SOCIAL UNREST.**

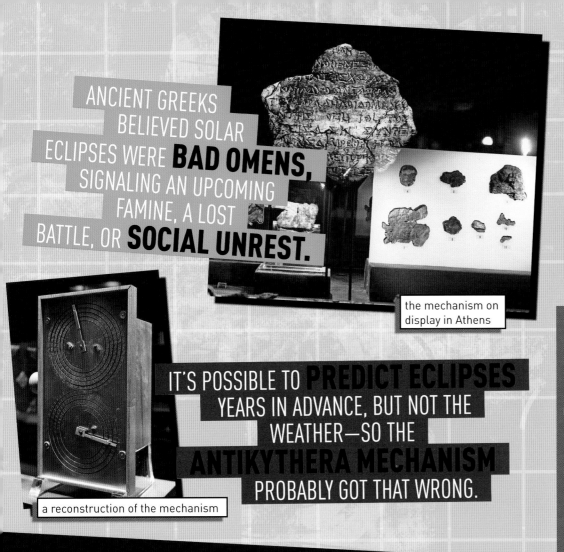

the mechanism on display in Athens

a reconstruction of the mechanism

IT'S POSSIBLE TO **PREDICT ECLIPSES** YEARS IN ADVANCE, BUT NOT THE WEATHER—SO THE **ANTIKYTHERA MECHANISM** PROBABLY GOT THAT WRONG.

Make It BETTER!

The Antikythera Mechanism used incredibly advanced technology to track and predict occurrences that were important to people of the time. And what's more, it did it all in a single device. If you could build a mechanism for use today, what events would you have it track? Would they all be related (such as occurrences in time in the Antikythera Mechanism), or would they be unrelated? If they were unrelated, how would all of the mechanisms work together in one device? Would your device help whole groups of people or just yourself?

The Antikythera Mechanism corroded in the ocean.

THE ANTIKYTHERA MECHANISM SEEMED **SO ADVANCED** FOR ITS TIME THAT SOME PEOPLE THOUGHT IT WAS BROUGHT TO EARTH BY SPACE ALIENS OR **TIME TRAVELERS!**

GOLDEN OLDIES

How have **FLUTES** shaped music around the world?

Dig In

Ah, the humble flute. If the word makes you think of a bunch of band members blowing into shiny metal tubes, you don't know the half of it. A flute may not be the biggest or loudest instrument in the school band, but it has a history and worldwide impact that no other instrument can claim. Tune in to find out why.

How does a flute make sound?

Why do they come in so many shapes?

How do you get different notes?

JUST THE FACTS

WORLD MUSIC

The flute is not just **the oldest** musical instrument in the world, it's also the only one found **all over the world.** Take a tour of the flute family.

All in the Family

The flute family is huge. It has relatives all over the world, members of all shapes and sizes, and ancestors going back at least 40,000 years, when saber-toothed cats and woolly mammoths roamed the Earth. But what all flutes have in common is how they make their whistling or birdsong sound: You blow air across a hole. Your breath hits the hole's edge, and the airstream rapidly flutters between blowing into the hole and blowing away from it. That's exactly what you want, because sound is produced when something—in this case, air—vibrates. Other wind instruments get their vibrations from "buzzing" reeds (like a clarinet) or your own lips (like a trumpet). But flutes are special.

Craft Work

Today's concert flute typically is made of metal—usually silver but sometimes gold or, rarely, platinum. But that's a modern innovation. The earliest flutes, dating back at least 40,000 years to the Paleolithic era, were made of hollow animal bones, especially bird wing bones, which are naturally strong and hollow. As our ancestors became more crafty, they began to carve flutes of ivory from mammoths, often in two pieces that fit together. Later, people fashioned flutes from clay or carved them from wood—traditional styles that still exist.

The **xun**, an egg-shaped Chinese vessel flute made of pottery, dates back to about 5000 B.C. They often have two to five finger holes and are shaped like fruit, fish, or other animals. The player blows across a hole at the top.

The **bansuri**, a side-blown flute often seen in ancient Buddhist and Hindu art, is traditionally made of bamboo with six or eight finger holes. Its lineage goes back to at least 1500 to 1200 B.C. The Hindu god Lord Krishna is considered a master of the bamboo flute.

The **pan flute** (panpipes), named after the Greek god Pan, dates back to 2000 to 3000 B.C. in ancient Greece. Versions of the instrument, played by blowing across the end of the tubes, are popular throughout the world.

The **ocarina** dates back over 12,000 years and was popular throughout Mesoamerica, Asia, and, later, Europe. It presumably got its name, "Little Goose," in the 1850s, when an Italian boy designed a vessel flute with a mouthpiece protruding from the side, looking a bit like a goose. It's played by blowing into it.

Today's Western **concert flute** was developed in the 19th century by Theobald Boehm, a German goldsmith, engineer, and musician. Dissatisfied with the limits of earlier flutes, he designed a system of keys to improve the instrument's sound and versatility.

Madagascar's **sodina** and the Southeast Asian **suling,** believed to be related, are simple end-blown flutes, often made of bamboo and varying in size. Though it's difficult to date their origins, their widespread use suggests they have deep roots.

The **first flutes**, dating back at least 40,000 years, were found in caves in southwestern Germany. Made of animal bones and mammoth ivory, they're the oldest known musical instruments.

FUN FACT

CHEYENNE MEN HISTORICALLY PLAYED FLUTES TO WIN THE HEARTS OF WOMEN THEY LOVED. IF THE RELATIONSHIP WAS MEANT TO BE, HIS BELOVED WOULD **FOLLOW THE FLUTE'S SONG** TO FIND HIM.

BLOWN OVER

Flutes produce sound when your breath hits a sharp edge, which makes the airstream vibrate. For side-blown flutes, you aim your breath across the edge of a hole. But end-blown flutes, like this Native American flute from the Cheyenne tradition, route your breath for you. Check out how they do this clever trick.

You blow into the end of the flute.

Your breath hits the splitting edge, rapidly forcing the airstream to flutter above and below the edge. That makes the air vibrate—producing sound.

The slow air chamber collects your breath and directs it out of the chamber.

A shallow channel, called the flue, routes the air to the sound hole.

The instrument's tube is partially blocked to create the flue.

ORCHESTRAL COUSINS

All instruments have families. They have big, extended families, including all winds (instruments you blow into), strings (instruments you pluck or bow), or percussion (instruments you strike or beat). And they have smaller, more immediate families. Winds include brass instruments—trumpets and the like—and woodwinds. The woodwind family is further divided into the reeds (such as clarinets and oboes) and, of course, our friends the flutes.

The mouthpiece of **END-BLOWN FLUTES**, with its thin channel that routes your breath against a sharp edge, has a special name: **FIPPLE.** Go on, impress your band teacher.

WANT TO KNOW MORE?

TELL ME MORE

OF NOTE

Flutes' delightful sounds start when your breath breaks on a splitting edge, but they don't end there. The sound waves travel into the sound chamber, where the sound's pitch—how high or low it is—can be changed. Yes, we're talking about making different notes. If you play, you know how: You press keys or cover or uncover finger holes to get them. What you're actually doing is changing how much of the instrument is used to make sound. When you cover all the holes on a long flute, you're using the entire flute. The sound waves have more room to vibrate, so they spread out and make a lower sound. If you open the holes, it's like you cut the tube off. The sound waves can only go as far as the hole. The shorter the distance, the faster they bounce around, so they make a higher pitch. Of course, how hard you blow and how you aim your breath also matter a lot!

FUN FACTS

● Peter Broderick won the 1955 **All-Ireland Flute Championship** on an instrument he made out of **copper pipe.**

● The **Library of Congress** in Washington, D.C., has the largest collection of flutes in the world—nearly 1,700, some dating back to the 16th century. The collection includes **flutes made of wood, gold,** and even **glass.**

● In central and northeastern New Guinea, large side-blown **bamboo flutes** can stretch over **six feet** (1.8 m) long. The sacred instruments are played by men for religious ceremonies.

The REAL DEAL

Imagine this: a bunch of Neanderthals sitting around the campfire and jamming on flutes. Preposterous? Maybe not! In 1995, an intriguing discovery was made in the Divje Babe Archaeological Park in Slovenia: a 43,000-year-old hollow cave-bear bone with well-placed holes punched along its length—just like a flute. Some archaeologists believe it's the oldest musical instrument ever found, one possibly made by Neanderthals. But it's hard to be 100 percent sure. The artifact is broken on both ends, so it's difficult to know what the rest of it looked like. Some archaeologists and musicologists believe it may have had four holes. They say the holes line up to play part of a musical scale. Someone even made a replica of it and played it. But other scientists aren't so sure. They believe the holes are actually teeth marks. They say some kind of carnivore was snacking on the dead cave bear and crunched through the bone. Scientists continue to study the find, but we may never know for sure. Take a look at the photographic evidence. What do you think? Flute or snack?

SOUND IDEA

Long, open-ended flutes and rounded vessel flutes seem totally different. But the way you get different notes on them is amazingly similar: You change how much of the instrument is available for making sound.

NATIVE AMERICAN FLUTE

When you cover the finger holes on an open-ended flute, like a Native American flute, the sound waves spread out in the whole tube and make a lower pitch. When you uncover the holes, it's like you're making the instrument smaller—at least as far as the sound waves are concerned. They bounce around faster and make a higher note.

OCARINA

When you cover the finger holes on a vessel flute, like an ocarina, the sound waves use the entire chamber and make a lower pitch. But when you uncover the holes, increasing the open area, the pitch gets higher. It's like you've removed some of the ocarina's chamber, and the air rushes out.

HIGHS AND LOWS

AMPLITUDE
Tall sound waves are louder than short sound waves.

FREQUENCY
Sound waves with frequent peaks are higher pitched than waves with fewer peaks.

Sound travels on waves—but the waves act differently depending on how loud or soft the sound is (its volume) or how high or low it is (its pitch). A sound's volume depends on the waves' height (its amplitude). A sound's pitch depends on how fast the waves vibrate (its frequency, meaning the number of waves that pass by in a second).

TRY THIS!

You don't need an expensive instrument to learn how to toot on a flute. Grab a bottle, lay your lower lip on the edge of the hole, and blow across the top, so only a little air goes inside the bottle. Just like learning how to play any instrument, it takes practice. Here's a tip: Instead of puckering up, pull the edges of your mouth back a little bit in the direction of your ears. Once you get a good sound, experiment making different tones by changing the amount of water inside the bottle.

POWER OF THE PRESS

How did Gutenberg's **PRINTING PRESS** start an information revolution?

Dig In

Today, when we're bombarded 24/7 with social media, news, podcasts, TV shows, and more, it's hard to imagine a time when information was hard to get. But that's how it was before the mid-1400s. It was a rare treat to get a book—and one few people could afford (assuming they could read in the first place). Gutenberg's printing press changed all that, spreading knowledge and putting books in the hands of everyday people. Bookworms, rejoice!

How did the printing press work **?**

Why was it such an important innovation **?**

What impact did it have on society **?**

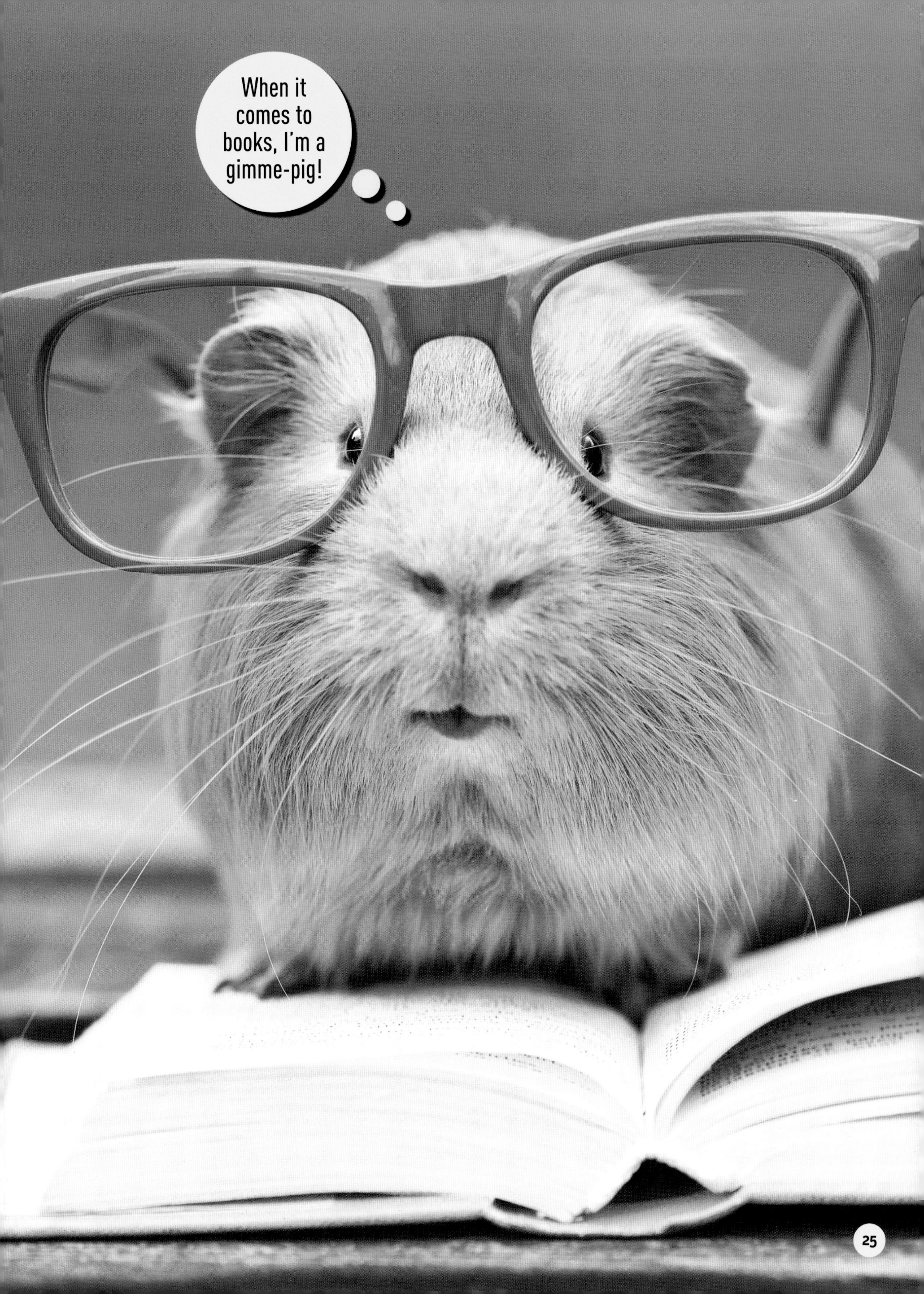
When it comes to books, I'm a gimme-pig!

JUST THE FACTS

Mass Appeal

The printing press, introduced by German goldsmith Johannes Gutenberg around 1452, was an amazing device that allowed books to be easily and quickly mass-produced, making them cheaper both to make and to buy. The machine used reusable metal type—individual letters and symbols—arranged to create whatever text needed to be printed. The person operating the press dabbed ink on the type, placed a sheet of paper on top of it, and slid it under a screw press. The press pushed down hard on the paper, leaving a crisp imprint of the letters on the paper. It could be used over and over to make many copies, as long as fresh ink was added.

Game Changer

Before Gutenberg's press, manuscripts in Europe were typically copied by hand and available only to the intellectual elite and wealthy upper classes. Some printers were using block-printing, carving entire words or pictures into a block of wood, and then inking it and transferring the image to paper. But that process was barely an improvement. It took a long time and cost a lot. Gutenberg's press was a faster and cheaper way to create books and pamphlets. It opened up learning and knowledge to everyone. Scientists, philosophers, church officials, and political leaders could share their ideas quickly with each other and with larger audiences. More and more people—not just the elites—learned to read. Libraries grew, and information spread widely. Gutenberg's press created an information revolution.

EVOLUTION OF TYPOGRAPHY

Typography, the style of letters used in printing, has changed a lot over the years. Since Gutenberg's time, it changed to become easier to read and to reflect the styles of the time, eventually even losing its serifs sometimes, the little "hats" and "feet" at the top and bottom of letters. Once the computer era arrived, thousands of different typefaces became available. Take a look at some of the typographical all-stars.

BLACKLETTER:
created by Gutenberg around 1448 to look like the hand-lettering of the time, it was pretty and bold, but dense and a bit hard to read.

ROMAN:
created in the 15th century by French typographer Nicolas Jenson, it was easier to read—and a big hit. It was inspired by lettering on ancient Roman buildings.

ITALICS:
a slanted, stylish typeface popularized by Italian typecutter Francesco Griffo and printer Aldus Manutius in 1501, it was designed to fit more letters on a page and save money.

CASLON TYPEFACE:
created by English engraver William Caslon in the early 1700s, it set a new standard for clarity, with uniform strokes and a thick serif. It's now classified as an "old style" typeface.

CASLON EGYPTIAN:
created by William Caslon IV around 1816, it was innovative for having no serifs. It took a while to catch on, but eventually sans-serif typefaces became very popular.

DIDONE:
emerging in the late 1700s, these typefaces had thin, long serifs and extreme differences between thick and thin strokes. They're now classified as "modern" typefaces.

BASKERVILLE:
inspired by Caslon, English type designer John Baskerville gained fame in the mid-1700s with his typeface, now classified as "transitional" with its thinner serifs and thick and thin strokes.

EGYPTIAN:
spurred by advertising in the late 19th century, many new typefaces—with taller letters or fatter letters—were created to use on posters and billboards.

FUTURA:
in the early 20th century, a backlash against the complexity of the advertising typefaces resulted in simpler typefaces based on geometric shapes.

GILL SANS:
created by British typeface designer Eric Gill in the early 1900s, the typeface featured gentler, more natural curves.

HELVETICA:
one of the world's most popular typefaces, it was created in 1957 by Max Miedinger in Switzerland. With simple curves, the typeface was available in many different thicknesses.

PAGE TURNER

Gutenberg's mechanical printing press, with its movable type, made it much easier and faster to print many copies of a book or pamphlet.

A long lever, which printers called the "devil's tail," made it easier to lower the screw press.

The inked type was covered with a sheet of paper and held in a frame that slid under the press.

The press pushed the paper down onto the type, pressing the ink into the paper.

A compositor arranged the type—individual letters and symbols—in a tray to make the text of a book. It could take a full day to make a single page of text, but it could be used to make many copies.

Horizontal guide rails, like train tracks, helped the type frame slide back and forth easily.

reusable wood-block type

WANT TO KNOW MORE?

TELL ME MORE

PUTTING IT ALL TOGETHER

Gutenberg didn't invent his printing press from scratch. He actually combined several other inventions and processes to create his amazing machine. Farmers had been using screw presses for centuries to squeeze the juice out of olives and grapes. Those agricultural presses provided the model for his printing press. Other printers already used wood-block printing and even some typesetting (the placement of characters on a page), but Gutenberg added movable type and better ink to make his printing press a groundbreaking success.

Myth vs. FACT

MYTH: Gutenberg was the "Father of Printing."

FACT: You can't say enough good things about Gutenberg's printing press. It sped ideas through Renaissance Europe, helped bring knowledge to everyday people, and created the original information age. In fact, the famous 17th-century English philosopher Francis Bacon (aka, Mr. "Knowledge is Power") said it was one of three inventions that "have changed the appearance and state of the whole world." The whole world! So, obviously, Gutenberg is the "Father of Printing," right? Wrong! The Chinese beat Gutenberg, and not by a little—by hundreds of years. They used a wood-block printing technique in the 6th and 7th centuries, and a few hundred years later even developed movable type. But it was hard to make the process work with Chinese, which has about 10,000 characters or more. It never caught on there. But in Gutenberg's Europe? No problem! The relatively simple alphabets of languages like German, English, and Latin were perfect for the printing press. Gutenberg recognized that, and he combined the typesetting technologies of Asia with presses used in Europe and modified the recipe for ink. His most original contribution was the letter mold. So, Gutenberg could be considered the "Father of Letter Molds," but that's not quite as catchy.

FUN FACTS

● Gutenberg has an **asteroid named after him.** Its official name is **777 Gutemberga,** and it orbits our sun. It was discovered in 1914 by German astronomer **Franz Kaiser.**

● Experts estimate that before Gutenberg's press, there were only about **30,000 books** in all of Europe. Less than 50 years later, that number had swelled to some **10 to 12 million.**

● The **printing press** wasn't Gutenberg's only business venture, it just made him **famous.** In fact, he designed the press after a failed attempt to **sell metal mirrors.** He hoped the press would help him **pay for those losses!**

BOOKMAKER

Gutenberg adapted several technologies and added his own innovations to make a printing press capable of mass-producing books and other printed materials.

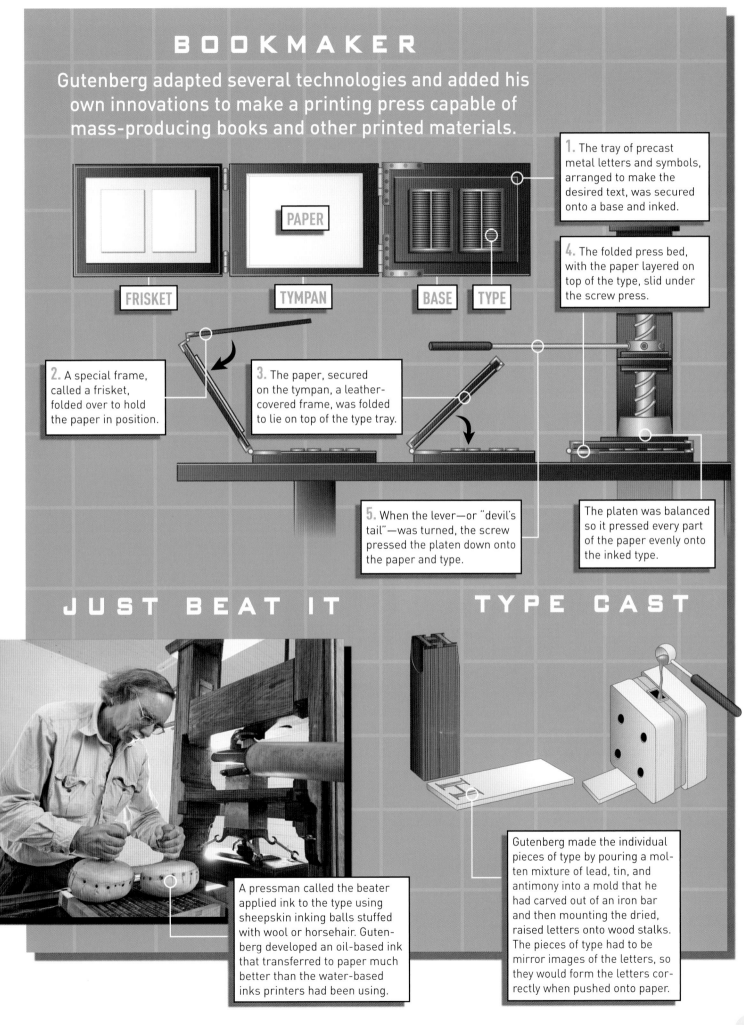

1. The tray of precast metal letters and symbols, arranged to make the desired text, was secured onto a base and inked.

4. The folded press bed, with the paper layered on top of the type, slid under the screw press.

FRISKET

PAPER

TYMPAN

BASE **TYPE**

2. A special frame, called a frisket, folded over to hold the paper in position.

3. The paper, secured on the tympan, a leather-covered frame, was folded to lie on top of the type tray.

5. When the lever—or "devil's tail"—was turned, the screw pressed the platen down onto the paper and type.

The platen was balanced so it pressed every part of the paper evenly onto the inked type.

JUST BEAT IT

TYPE CAST

A pressman called the beater applied ink to the type using sheepskin inking balls stuffed with wool or horsehair. Gutenberg developed an oil-based ink that transferred to paper much better than the water-based inks printers had been using.

Gutenberg made the individual pieces of type by pouring a molten mixture of lead, tin, and antimony into a mold that he had carved out of an iron bar and then mounting the dried, raised letters onto wood stalks. The pieces of type had to be mirror images of the letters, so they would form the letters correctly when pushed onto paper.

PROFILE: Guillermo de Anda

UNDERWATER ARCHAEOLOGIST

Guillermo de Anda is a detective. He pieces together clues, follows trails, and solves mysteries. He just happens to do it by dangling from 100-foot (30 m) rappel lines or scuba diving into hidden, underwater caves.

"I do really have the coolest job in the world," he says. "It's a perfect combination of extreme sports, adventure, mystery, science."

Guillermo is an expert on the ancient Maya, a great Mesoamerican civilization perhaps best known for their stepped-pyramid temples and

" IT'S A PERFECT COMBINATION OF EXTREME SPORTS, ADVENTURE, MYSTERY, SCIENCE. "

palaces, like at Chichén Itzá, and their knowledge of math and astronomy. Like other archaeologists, Guillermo studies the ancient civilization by uncovering their important sites and analyzing artifacts, bones, and other remains.

But while most archaeologists work aboveground, Guillermo goes under it. He explores important Maya sites in caves and cenotes, flooded caves or natural sinkholes, in Yucatán, Mexico. "They had a strong symbolism for the ancient Maya, and they both represented the same: the entrance to the underworld, to the sacred world, to the world of the supernatural," he explains. "We know that going into those holes we're going to find cool stuff."

The ancient Maya wanted to make it difficult to find these religious sites—and that's exactly how Guillermo likes it. The harder the sites are to find, the better their findings. But it takes incredible detective work to discover them.

FOLLOWING THE CLUES

Guillermo spent five years connecting clues he found in ancient Maya texts and in detailed, 450-year-old accounts of the Spanish Inquisition. The Spaniards interrogated the Maya to learn where they performed human sacrifices—a ritual the Spaniards wanted to stop.

Guillermo was the first archaeologist to connect the Maya and Spanish texts with mysterious remains discovered in caves. He traveled to remote villages and asked about cenotes mentioned in the accounts. To his amazement, some of the village elders knew about the places and led him to the sacred sites.

What he discovered blew his mind.

UNDERWATER JOURNEY

The Maya had altered a series of sacred caves and cenotes to mimic the arduous journey they believed spirits would travel to Xibalba, the Maya underworld. Guillermo and his team followed the path, squeezing through narrow tunnels, crawling through snakes and scorpions, and dodging swarms of bats. They went through chambers described in the Maya's sacred texts: a "room of knives" filled with sharp stones and stalactites and a "chamber of shaking cold," where icy surface air gusted through the cavern. Along the way, they found submerged pyramids, temples behind hidden doorways, altars with traces of burnt offerings, and a fantastic mural of mythical animals: a jaguar, deer, and bird.

Guillermo is often the first person to see artifacts that have lain undisturbed for hundreds, maybe even thousands, of years. The treasures he finds in the cenotes are perfectly preserved in the deep freshwater environment, which stays a constant temperature, untouched by light or waves.

He is still awed when he descends into a cave or cenote and thinks of the ancient Maya worshipping at the site, surrounded by all its beauty. "They were there, and they found divinity there."

ON A CHILDHOOD TRIP WITH HIS UNCLE TO A MUSEUM IN MEXICO CITY, GUILLERMO WAS FASCINATED BY A DISPLAY OF HUMAN SKULLS. HE DIDN'T JUST THINK THEY WERE COOL, HE WANTED TO KNOW WHAT HAD HAPPENED TO THE PEOPLE.

Four skulls are among the remains that fascinate Guillermo.

A **RESEARCHER** AT THE INSTITUTO NACIONAL DE ANTROPOLOGÍA E HISTORIA, GUILLERMO HAS A DOCTORATE IN **MESOAMERICAN STUDIES,** A MASTER'S IN **SKELETAL ANTHROPOLOGY,** AND A BACHELOR'S DEGREE IN **ARCHAEOLOGY.**

Guillermo rappels into cenotes.

This flute is one artifact that has been found in a cave.

IN 2012, GUILLERMO BECAME THE FIRST MEXICAN ARCHAEOLOGIST TO BE APPOINTED A NATIONAL GEOGRAPHIC EMERGING EXPLORER.

Guillermo dives into cenotes that were important to the ancient Maya.

BITS OF MAGIC

How does the LYCURGUS CUP pull off its color-changing trick?

Dig In

Imagine something so tiny that it's 80,000 to 100,000 times smaller than the width of one of your hairs. Scientists and engineers actually work on that scale, the nanoscale. It's super-advanced and cutting-edge stuff. So imagine how scientists felt when they discovered that the ancient Romans used nanotechnology 1,600 years ago to make a chalice change colors! Minds. Blown. Want to know how they did it?

How does the cup change color **?**

Where does the red color come from **?**

How does nanotechnology fit in **?**

JUST THE FACTS

LIGHT SHOW

Ahead of Its Time

The Lycurgus Cup, a fancy glass chalice likely made in Rome in the fourth century A.D., changes color depending on how light hits it. Under normal light, it's a peaceful jade green. But if you shine a white light source through it, it glows an angry red. For years, the chalice's color-changing trick baffled scientists, but in 1990, researchers discovered that teeny particles of gold and silver were embedded in the glass. The particles were as small as 50 nanometers. It'd take a clump of a thousand of them to equal the size of a grain of table salt. When light hits the particles, they change the color of the cup. It was nanotechnology at its most brilliant.

Don't Tick Off a Greek God

The Lycurgus Cup has an amazing carving drawn from Greek mythology. It shows Lycurgus, a Thracian king from back around 800 B.C. Lycurgus had anger-management issues. He attacked the god Dionysus and his follower Ambrosia. Not a good idea! Ambrosia called out to Mother Earth, who transformed her into a vine. She snared the king and held him captive so that Dionysus and his buddies could punish him for his bad behavior.

Under normal light, the chalice is an opaque green.

When light shines through the cup, it glows red.

Lycurgus

The **LYCURGUS CUP** must have seemed like magic in the fourth century. In case you don't remember events back then, the **ROMAN EMPIRE** controlled much of western Europe and northern Africa. Roman leaders had been persecuting the young Christian Church for about **300 YEARS** but had a change of heart and adopted Christianity as the Roman state religion in 380.

Dionysus

FUN FACT

THE LYCURGUS CUP IS KNOWN AS A **"CAGE-CUP."** THE ARTWORK WAS CUT OUT OF THE GLASS, SO THE FIGURES LOOK KIND OF LIKE STATUES ATTACHED BY **TINY BRIDGES** TO THE CUP'S SURFACE.

The little metallic particles in the cup's glass are picky. They scatter blue and green light—colors that have relatively short wavelengths compared to other colors we can see. The scattering effect gives the cup a greenish color most of the time. So under normal light, it reflects the green color back to you. But if you shine white light through the cup, an interesting thing happens. When the light hits the metallic particles, the little electrons inside them get excited and jiggle a lot. They jiggle so much that they create a kind of screen that blocks the shorter blue and green waves but lets the red shine through.

FILTER EFFECT

Under normal light, the Lycurgus Cup's natural greenish color is reflected back to us. But when white light shines through it, the metallic nanoparticles in the glass scatter the shorter wavelengths of green and blue colors and let longer red wavelengths shine through. It makes the cup look red!

Whoa ... SLOW DOWN!
A Closer Look at Color

What's all this about light waves? To really understand how the Lycurgus Cup glows red, we need to get into the details about light. Light can behave like a wave. Different colors of light have different wavelengths. The colors at the reddish end of a rainbow have longer wavelengths than those at the bluish end. (A fun way to remember the order of the rainbow—red, orange, yellow, green, blue, indigo, violet—is to spell the name ROY G. BIV.) When we see something, we're actually seeing the light that bounces off that object and into our eyes. If we see a red bike, it means the bike bounced red light toward us but absorbed all the other colors of light. That's kind of how the Lycurgus Cup pulls off its trick.

FUN FACTS

● The **Lycurgus Cup** inspired University of Illinois researchers to create a novel light-sensitive sensor that has a **billion teeny-tiny dents** coated with gold and silver nanoparticles. It's like a billion little Lycurgus Cups.

● Scientists suspect that the Lycurgus Cup didn't only change color in the light. **Different types of liquid** poured into it may have triggered the **color change,** too. Fun party trick!

TRY THIS!

Light is not like paint. When you mix a bunch of paint colors together, you get a muddy brown. When you mix all colors of light together, you get white. Want to see for yourself? Try this experiment. Cut a big circle out of a white paper plate or card stock. Use a pencil and ruler to divide the circle into three equal pie-shaped sections, and color the sections red, green, and blue. Use a pencil or pen tip to punch small holes about one inch (3 cm) to the right and left of the exact center of your circle. Take about a yard (or meter) of string and thread each end through a hole, and then tie the loose ends together to make a loop. Hold each end of the loop, center the circle on the string, and twist the circle round and round to wind the string tightly. (You'll need to anchor one end of the loop somehow or get an extra hand for that part.) Pull the twisted ends of the string apart so the string quickly unwinds and spins the circle. What happens to the colors?

HIGH FLIER

How did the FIRST POWERED AIRSHIP take flight?

Dig In

In 1852, half a century before the Wright brothers made their historic flight, French inventor Henri Giffard lifted off in the first powered airship, a dirigible. He proved it was possible to navigate the skies—and not just drift along on the wind, like the hot-air balloons that inspired his craft. Climb aboard to see why this invention wasn't just a flight of fancy.

How did it get off the ground ?

What powered the aircraft ?

How could you steer the dirigible ?

JUST THE FACTS

Rising Star

Here was the challenge: to design an aircraft that was lighter-than-air but propelled by something other than the wind. Hot-air balloons had shown that hydrogen, a gas lighter than air, could lift aircraft. But propulsion stumped many inventors. Some came up with human-powered designs, with long oars to paddle through the air or hand-cranks to turn propellers. But engineer Henri Giffard realized he needed to put an engine on board.

Liftoff

Giffard took the basic design for his 144-foot (44-m)-long steerable, or dirigible, balloon from a model he had seen a couple years earlier. The dirigible was cigar-shaped to cut down on wind resistance and filled with hydrogen gas. To pilot the airship, Giffard built a small steam engine to power a rear-facing three-bladed propeller and added a sail-shaped rudder to steer it. In 1852, Giffard flew his steam-powered airship 17 miles (27 km) from Paris to Elancourt, France, at a speed of six miles an hour (10 km/h). No one was able to improve on his design for two decades.

AIRSHIP PIONEERS

Powered airships became a popular means of air travel in the early 1900s, but **design flaws** led to their downfall. Improved, safer designs are letting powered airships make a comeback.

1852: The first powered dirigible, built by French engineer Henri Giffard, takes to the skies.

1900: The first zeppelin, the LZ-1 airship, flies with German count Ferdinand von Zeppelin piloting. But the hydrogen-filled airship is too heavy, underpowered, and hard to control.

1908: The much-improved LZ-4 flies for 12 hours over Switzerland, impressing the public. When a freak accident destroys it later in the year, people raise money for Count Zeppelin to continue building airships.

1919: A fleet of Goodyear Blimps takes to the sky, largely to advertise the company name.

1931: The U.S.S. *Akron,* the U.S. Navy's "flying aircraft carrier" built by Goodyear-Zeppelin, takes to the skies. Capable of carrying up to five fighter planes, it hangs a trapeze from its belly to launch and recover the planes while flying. It crashes two years later. Its sister ship, the U.S.S. *Macon,* suffers a similar fate.

1929: The British-built R101, which is 735 feet (224 m) long, becomes the biggest airship in the world. It crashes the next year and explodes. Its sister ship, the R100, is grounded.

1928: The *Graf Zeppelin,* the most successful zeppelin, starts its nine-year, 590-flight career. It sparks international interest in zeppelins, but Hitler's Nazi regime later uses it for propaganda, showing Germany's "superiority."

1925: Goodyear's *Pilgrim* is the first commercial nonrigid airship lifted by helium, a safer gas than the hydrogen used in the German and British airships.

1936: The *Hindenburg,* at 804 feet (245 m) long, becomes the largest object ever to fly—still. At first a propaganda tool for the Nazi government, it later begins luxury flights between Germany and the United States. Its fiery crash in 1937 ends the age of the rigid airship.

1950s: Goodyear Blimps begin aerial coverage of sporting events in the United States.

1995: The Aeros 50, a 78-foot (24-m)-long advertising blimp, takes to the skies, lifted by helium.

2006: The Lockheed Martin P-791 airship takes its first flight. It's intended to carry cargo.

2012: The Airlander 10, the world's largest existing aircraft at 302 feet (92 m) in length, begins secret test flights. The airship, built by Hybrid Air Vehicles in England, may be used for military or civilian flight.

BALLOON BEATER

Henri Giffard's powered airship proved it was possible to fly a "dirigible balloon" wherever you wanted—no matter where the wind blew.

BALLOON
The cigar shape of the balloon decreased wind resistance, allowing the dirigible to sail through the air without being buffeted too much by winds.

PROPELLER
The three-bladed propeller, turned by the engine's power, pushed the dirigible forward.

SAIL RUDDER
A movable, triangular-shaped sail acted as a rudder to steer the aircraft.

ENGINE
A small steam engine provided the power.

Giffard is one of the 72 great scientists whose names are inscribed on the **EIFFEL TOWER** in Paris.

WANT TO KNOW MORE?

TELL ME MORE

POWER UP

To power his dirigible, Henri Giffard built the smallest, lightest steam engine ever made at the time. But it was still 250 pounds (113 kg) and needed a 100-pound (45-kg) boiler plus fuel to fire it! The engine produced just a little bit more power than today's steam irons—the gadgets people use to get wrinkles out of their clothes. But since the engine only needed to push the aircraft, and not help lift it, it got the job done—but only barely.

SAFETY FIRST

The biggest concern was using a steam engine around hydrogen, a highly flammable gas (that led to the *Hindenburg* disaster). The engine was powered by burning coke, a fuel made from coal (not the soft drink!), and Giffard needed to make sure burning cinders wouldn't escape from the engine and ignite the gas. Back in his day, steam engines had smokestacks on their tops, but Giffard created a long exhaust tube that directed sparks down and behind the balloon.

Whoa ... SLOW DOWN!
A Closer Look at Buoyancy

How can a balloon or dirigible rise up and float in the air? It comes down to a force called buoyancy. (You may have heard of it in terms of boats being able to float.) Air and other gases—like liquids—push up against any object immersed in them. If a dirigible weighs less than the air it displaces (the air that would occupy the same space if the blimp weren't there), it'll float. Of course, a dirigible with its fabric, engine, passenger, and so on, weighs more than air. But that's where the gas inside the dirigible matters. The "lifting gas" inside a dirigible is lighter than air. We don't usually think of air having weight, but it does—like everything else on Earth. Different gases have different weights, and hydrogen and helium—the two main "lifting gases"—are both really light. Their molecules aren't packed together as closely as air's. In fact, helium is seven times less dense than air, and hydrogen is 14 times less dense. If you put enough helium into a balloon, the combined weight of the gas and balloon will be less than the same volume of air.

The Airlander, the world's largest existing aircraft, is as long as a football field.

MOVING ON

Giffard's expertise in steam power let him succeed where others had failed: creating the first powered airship with a source of propulsion and a way to change direction.

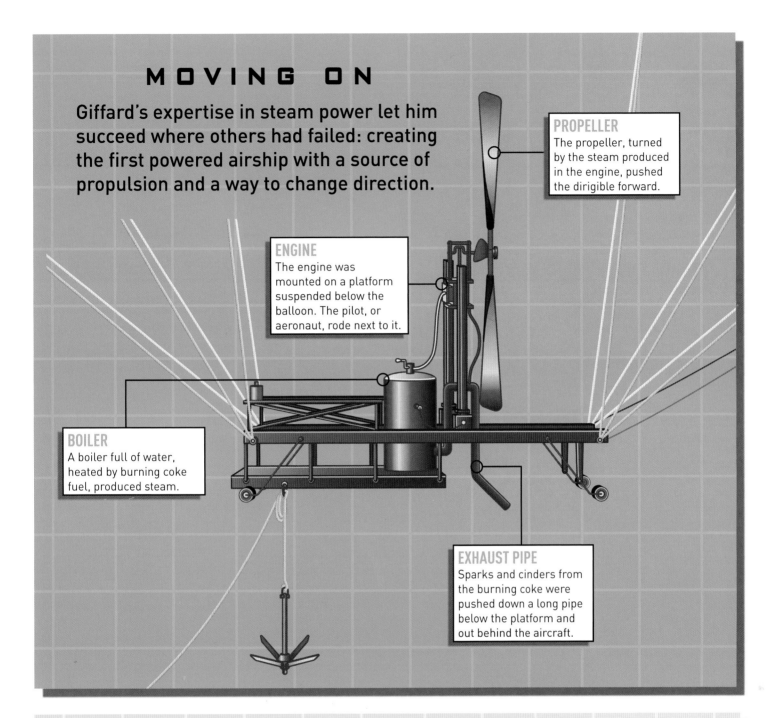

PROPELLER
The propeller, turned by the steam produced in the engine, pushed the dirigible forward.

ENGINE
The engine was mounted on a platform suspended below the balloon. The pilot, or aeronaut, rode next to it.

BOILER
A boiler full of water, heated by burning coke fuel, produced steam.

EXHAUST PIPE
Sparks and cinders from the burning coke were pushed down a long pipe below the platform and out behind the aircraft.

FUN FACTS

● "Dirigible" may not have been the **most creative** name for Giffard's invention, but it definitely was accurate. The word **"dirigible"** comes from the Latin word *dirige*, which means "to direct or **to steer.**"

● **After** his groundbreaking dirigible, Henri Giffard built another airship and a series of **large balloons.** He paid for them using money he made from his **other inventions,** including an injector that fed water into steam engines.

● Airships come in different varieties: nonrigid airships, like **blimps,** which only use gas to puff the balloon out; **semirigid airships,** which have a stiff support running the balloon's length to help hold its shape; and **rigid airships,** like the *Graf Zeppelin*, which have an internal skeleton to keep their shape.

TRY THIS!

GET YOUR BEARINGS

MAKE YOUR OWN COMPASS

Long before map apps and GPS, ship captains relied on compasses to sail the seven seas. Maybe you've taken a compass on a hike or used one in an orienteering camp to find north. The ancestor of that clever little device goes back 2,000 years, when the Chinese created a spoon-shaped "south-pointer" on a bronze plate. That first compass was used just for fortune-telling—mainly finding the best time and place for events like burials! But by the early 11th century, Chinese trading ships navigated to faraway lands with the help of compasses suspended in water. In this experiment, you'll follow in their footsteps by making your own working water compass. Get ready to set sail!

WHAT YOU NEED

TIME: about 20 minutes

A grown-up's help if you use any sharp things

1. Metal sewing needle about 1 or 2 inches (2.5 to 5 cm) long or small metal (uncoated) paper clip

2. Magnet (a strong one from a hardware store is best, but even a fridge magnet can work)

3. Cork piece, like from a wine bottle or a really thick memo board, or Styrofoam piece

4. Scissors or a hobby knife, like an X-Acto knife

5. Tape (preferably a waterproof kind like duct tape)

6. Pliers (optional)

7. Wire cutters (optional)

8. Wide glass or bowl

9. Water

NOTE: Keep the magnet away from electronic devices, like computers or cell phones, and credit cards—especially if you have the strong kind of magnet.

1. IF YOU'RE USING a paper clip, straighten it out and then break it (or cut it, if you have wire cutters) in the middle. To break it, fold it in half and unfold it several times until the metal gets so fatigued that it breaks. Pliers help with this step!

2. RUB YOUR MAGNET down the length of your needle or paper clip at least six times with a strong magnet or 12 to 20 times with a fridge magnet. Important: Always rub the same direction, not back and forth! If you're using a needle, rub from the "eye" to the point.

3. CUT A SMALL circle from the cork or Styrofoam, about the size of four quarters stacked together, roughly 1/4 inch (0.6 cm) thick. If you're using a utility knife, have your grown-up do this step.

4. LAY THE CORK/STYROFOAM "coin" (or disk) on a flat surface.

5. LAY YOUR NEEDLE or straightened paper clip part on top of the coin, in the center, with about the same amount sticking out on each side. Use a little piece of tape to hold it in place.

6. PUT SOME WATER in your glass or bowl. Fill about halfway.

7. GENTLY PLACE your cork/Styrofoam-and-needle pointer on the water. Keep it floating in the center of the water, away from the sides of your glass or bowl.

8. PUT YOUR COMPASS on a flat surface and watch what happens. **TIP:** Make sure your magnet and tools are not near the glass or bowl.

9. EXPERIMENT: Once the needle is still, move your magnet near the compass and see how the needle reacts. How close does the magnet need to be to make the needle move? Try doing the experiment with a nail or other steel object (such as your pliers).

10. EXPERIMENT SOME MORE: If you have both a strong magnet from the hardware store and a flat refrigerator magnet, make a couple of compasses and see which one works better. Or try different ways to make a water compass; for example, try laying a needle or straightened paper clip on top of a floating leaf in still water.

THE NEEDLE IN YOUR COMPASS SHOULD LINE UP WITH EARTH'S NORTH AND SOUTH MAGNETIC POLES. (IF YOU'RE USING A NEEDLE, THE SHARP POINT MAY POINT EITHER NORTH OR SOUTH.) WHEN YOU BRING A MAGNET (OR OTHER MAGNETIZED METAL) NEAR YOUR COMPASS, THE POINTER SHOULD ROTATE TOWARD THAT MAGNET.

IT'S NOT MAGIC, IT'S MAGNETISM. WHEN YOU RUBBED YOUR MAGNET ALONG YOUR NEEDLE OR PAPER CLIP, YOU MAGNETIZED IT, TURNING IT INTO A WEAK MAGNET (BUT ONLY FOR A LITTLE WHILE). BECAUSE MAGNETS INTERACT WITH EACH OTHER (PULLING TOGETHER OR PUSHING APART), YOUR NEEDLE INTERACTS WITH EARTH'S WEAK MAGNETIC FIELD. FLOATING THE POINTER ON WATER LETS IT ROTATE TO LINE UP WITH EARTH'S MAGNETIC FIELD, SO ONE END POINTS NORTH AND THE OTHER POINTS SOUTH.

CHAPTER 2

OUT OF THIS WORLD

WE'RE PUSHING INTO THE FINAL FRONTIER.

That's right, space. We Earthlings are explorers. We want to know what else is out there—and if we're alone in the universe. Just one problem: We're designed for Earth—gravity, oxygen, those kinds of things. But no worries, engineers and scientists have us covered. They're finding ways for us to snooze our way into deep space, explore planets with jet packs, and colonize Mars. And they'll make sure cutting-edge space suits and robot helpers make it easy for us. Check out the cool tech that'll take us into the final frontier. It's out of this world. Really.

FLYING SOLO

How can JET PACKS let astronauts zip through space?

Dig In

Flying through outer space with only a jet pack on your back, no cords tethering you to a spacecraft. For many people, that's the dream image of space exploration. Too bad it's more fiction than fact. Jet packs have been too hard to control to be a serious explorer's tool. But that could soon change. Hop aboard and learn how next-generation jet packs may turn those dreams into reality.

How do you steer a jet pack?

Can they keep astronauts right-side up?

What can you do wearing one?

Earth must
be around here
somewhere ...

JUST THE FACTS

Getting a Boost

Jet packs are like overgrown backpacks with little rockets attached. When you want to go somewhere, you fire up the thrusters (the rockets), and they push you through space. That's where jet packs excel. But if you need to hold still in microgravity, well, that's a lot tougher. The thrusters have to fire this way and that way—burning lots of fuel—just to keep you in one place. And if you want to repair a satellite or knock a sample off an asteroid, good luck! When your hammer strikes the rock, you could be thrown, tumbling backward. (It's physics: For every action, there's an equal and opposite reaction. Your hammer goes one way, so you go the other.)

Fine Tuning

The next generation of jet packs may give astronauts more control—and even let them get some work done outside their spacecraft. These jet packs may include advanced gyroscopes, devices that resist tilting, and micro-thrusters to keep astronauts stable. The gyroscopes and micro-thrusters would work together with computer software, taking continual readouts of the astronaut's position and adjusting as needed. They'd let astronauts do some serious scientific exploration.

NOT JUST FOR SPACE

Jet packs are a popular way to get around—at least **in stories!** For nearly a century, **writers have dreamed up** various jet packs that could propel us around, both in space and on Earth. Check out these sweet rides.

1928: The character Richard Seaton, in *The Skylark of Space*, straps on a harness "to which were attached numerous handles, switches, boxes and other pieces of apparatus" and zips through the air, circling, looping, and making figure eights.

1928: Anthony "Buck" Rogers, hero of stories and comics, floats through the air wearing a "floater" belt, powered by a rocket encased in the mysterious element "inertron."

1949: Rocket Man, who appeared in a series of *King of the Rocket Men* movies, zipped around with an atomic-powered jet pack to fight evildoers, such as the evil genius Dr. Vulcan.

1965: In the movie *Thunderball*, James Bond, the suave Agent 007, escapes a pair of bad guys by donning a rocket belt and flying over a building—and he doesn't even wrinkle his suit.

1960s: The crew of the Jupiter 2, in TV's sci-fi series *Lost in Space*, uses rocket belts to explore new planets and to escape hostile encounters.

1982: *The Rocketeer* graphic novel, by Dave Stevens, features a pilot who flies with a prototype rocket pack. The hero took to the big screen in 1991 in a movie by the same name.

FUN FACT

IN 1961, HAROLD GRAHAM MADE THE FIRST UNTETHERED FLIGHT WEARING A JET-PROPELLED **"ROCKET BELT"** ON EARTH. HE FLEW ABOUT FOUR FEET (1.2 M) OFF THE GROUND **FOR 100 FEET** (30 M).

ROCKET PACK

An awesome jet pack, the manned maneuvering unit, allowed space shuttle astronauts to go on space walks in the 1980s without being tethered to their spacecraft.

THRUSTERS
At each of eight corners of the jet pack, a group of three nozzles (pointing different directions) fired to provide the thrust that propelled the astronaut in any direction.

GAS RESERVOIR
Two large tanks held nitrogen gas to fuel the jet pack. Tubes carried the fuel from the tanks to the thruster nozzles.

HAND CONTROLLERS
Astronauts used their fingertips to operate controllers at the end of the jet pack's two arms. The right-hand control handled rotation, while the left-hand control took care of acceleration.

LOCATOR LIGHT
The jet pack included lights to help the astronauts' visibility in space.

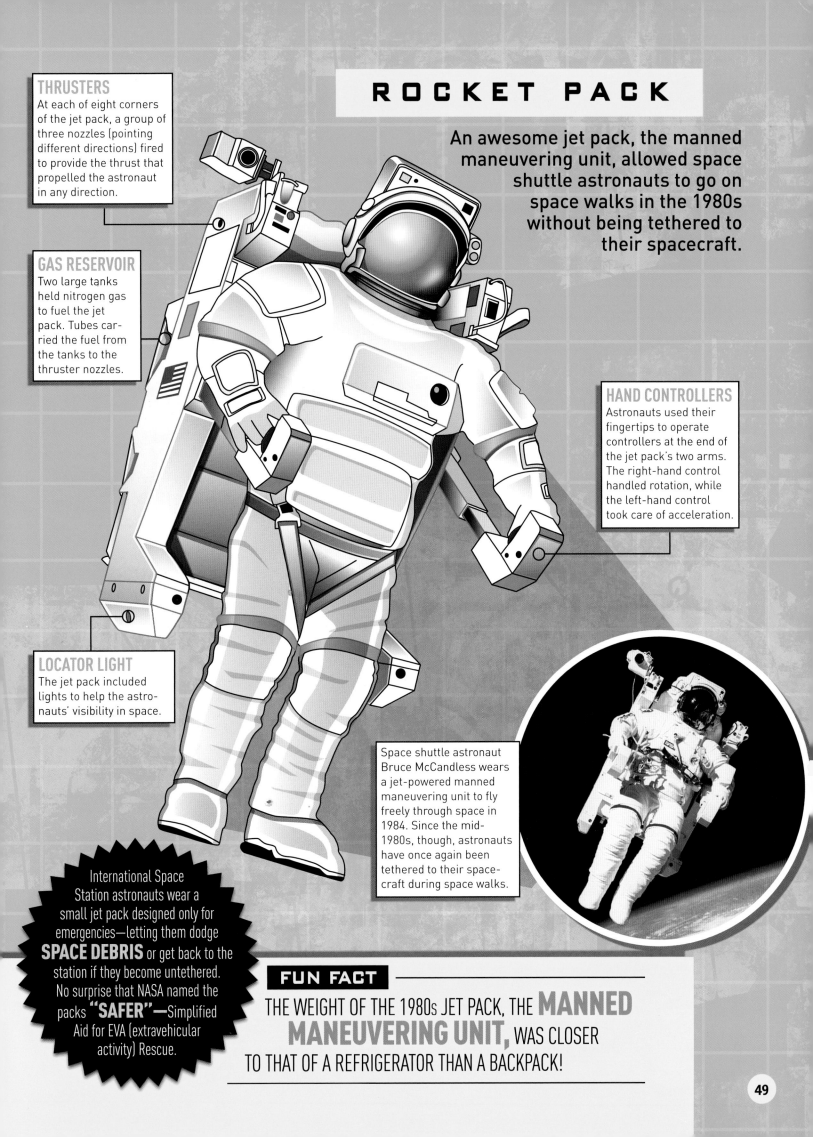

Space shuttle astronaut Bruce McCandless wears a jet-powered manned maneuvering unit to fly freely through space in 1984. Since the mid-1980s, though, astronauts have once again been tethered to their spacecraft during space walks.

International Space Station astronauts wear a small jet pack designed only for emergencies—letting them dodge **SPACE DEBRIS** or get back to the station if they become untethered. No surprise that NASA named the packs **"SAFER"**—Simplified Aid for EVA (extravehicular activity) Rescue.

FUN FACT
THE WEIGHT OF THE 1980s JET PACK, THE **MANNED MANEUVERING UNIT,** WAS CLOSER TO THAT OF A REFRIGERATOR THAN A BACKPACK!

TELL ME MORE

CONTROL FREAKS

The secret to the newest generation jet pack's control is how the gyroscopes work together. Each jet pack would have probably four advanced gyroscopes, called control moment gyroscopes. Each gyroscope would point a different direction and control the rotation—or resistance to rotation—in that direction. Working together, they'd have every direction covered. They'd be mounted to a frame on motorized pivots, so they'd adjust to whatever motion an astronaut made. Even chipping away rock samples. No more tumbling backward!

MAKING PROGRESS

NASA had experimented with gyroscope-equipped jet packs in the 1970s, but the gyroscopes back then were too heavy and power-hungry. Today's lighter, more efficient gyroscopes are more advanced.

Whoa ... SLOW DOWN!
A Closer Look at Gyroscopes

How can little gyroscopes keep a big astronaut stable? To answer that question, let's peek inside the device. At the heart of a gyroscope is a little wheel that spins really fast around its axis. It wants to keep spinning that same direction, no matter what. Again, it's a physics thing: The wheel has momentum—how strongly it's moving that way—and it'll keep going that way unless something messes with it. If you've ever played with a small gyroscope, you've probably seen that in action. You get the gyroscope spinning and give it a little bump. It jiggles a bit and goes right back to what it was doing.

TEST TIME

Engineers from Draper Laboratory and the Massachusetts Institute of Technology (MIT) test a gyroscope pack on NASA's "Vomit Comet," a special airplane that simulates microgravity. The gyroscopes could keep jet packs stable while astronauts work outside their spacecraft.

SPIN MASTER

A gyroscope puts physics to work in a handy device. The next-generation jet pack could use four of these marvels to give astronauts enough control to explore space freely.

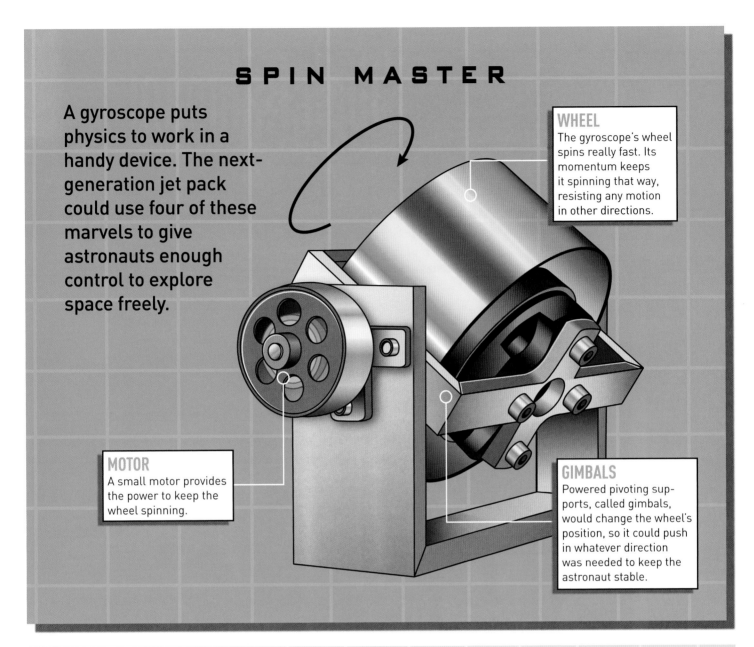

WHEEL
The gyroscope's wheel spins really fast. Its momentum keeps it spinning that way, resisting any motion in other directions.

MOTOR
A small motor provides the power to keep the wheel spinning.

GIMBALS
Powered pivoting supports, called gimbals, would change the wheel's position, so it could push in whatever direction was needed to keep the astronaut stable.

FUN FACTS

• You've probably played with a **gyroscope**—even without knowing it! Yo-yos, flying disks, footballs, and fidget spinners all use a gyroscopic spinning motion to **keep them stable.**

• A science officer on the **International Space Station** created a stable gyroscope out of three personal compact-disc players held together at different angles with **duct tape!** CD players spin the music discs inside, creating gyroscopic **stability.**

• Using gyroscopes in space is nothing new. **Spacecraft,** including the International Space Station, have used the advanced gyroscopes for decades to **keep stable.**

PROFILE: Hibah Rahmani

NASA ENGINEER

From early on, Hibah Rahmani was fascinated with the night sky.

"My fondest memory growing up is taking walks with my family at night, either in the desert or on the sidewalk by the Arabian (Persian) Gulf, looking up at the sky to admire the moon and stars," she says. She wondered what it was like for astronaut Neil Armstrong to walk on the moon.

And she wondered if she, too, could work to uncover the mysteries of space. It was a big dream for a young Pakistani girl growing up in Kuwait. And at times it seemed very, very far away.

> ## "IT WAS A BIG DREAM FOR A PAKISTANI GIRL GROWING UP IN KUWAIT."

EYES ON THE SKY

It was August 1990, and 10-year-old Hibah and her family had to flee their home, because Iraqi troops had invaded Kuwait. They took a bus westward across the desert to safety.

They arrived late at night at a refugee camp in a region known as "no-man's land" near the border between Jordan and Iraq. The camp was flooded with refugees, and all the tents already were taken. There was no shelter for Hibah's family.

"We had to sleep on the cold desert sand that night," Hibah recalls. "Even though it was a tough time for us, one of the memories that I have from that night is looking up at the beautiful dark sky, the golden moon, and the stars. It reminded me of my goals and dreams."

After leaving Kuwait, her family stayed in Pakistan, the country of Hibah's birth, for a couple years until it was safe to return to Kuwait. Hibah finished high school, then moved to the United States to study computer engineering at the University of Central Florida.

Hibah was a science whiz and breezed through high school in Kuwait. When she got to college, it was a lot harder. She failed her first physics exam. But she knew she had come too far to fail. "I spent a lot of time in the library," she says. "I went there, spent hours reading physics books, practicing problems. My grade slowly started to improve in the class."

The only way she could earn an A in the course was to answer every question right on the big, final exam. She had never done that before. "But I was going to give it my best shot," she says.

After the exam, she waited anxiously for her grade. She didn't see "100" written on the page. She saw "105"! She got everything right—plus a bonus question.

But the grade wasn't as important as the lesson Hibah learned from the experience. She knew she could do anything if she kept working at it.

PURSUING HER DREAMS

Hibah's hard work paid off. After she earned her degree in engineering, she got a job testing out parts that would go to the International Space Station. Sometimes astronauts would come by, and she soon began to dream about working at NASA.

She earned a master's degree in electrical and computer engineering and landed a job at the space agency. As an engineer at NASA's Kennedy Space Center, Hibah helps make sure rockets get safely into space. She's responsible for their electronic components, such as flight computers. But the best part of the job is seeing a rocket launch.

Hibah's life taught her never to give up—and that's advice she hopes others will follow. "What I learned from this entire experience is that no matter how difficult your circumstances are, you should always continue to stay focused on your goals and dream big," she says. "If I can do it, you can do it."

Spending time near the Persian Gulf was a fun pastime for Hibah.

NASA AND BOEING HAVE GIVEN HIBAH SEVERAL **AWARDS** FOR HER **GREAT WORK.**

WHEN SHE'S NOT HELPING **LAUNCH ROCKETS** INTO SPACE, HIBAH **LOVES TO PAINT** WITH WATERCOLORS AND GO SCUBA DIVING.

Hibah was always a math and science whiz.

The SpaceX Falcon 9 rocket is one of the rockets Hibah works with.

HIBAH DOESN'T **ONLY THINK** ABOUT SPACE. SHE ALSO HELPS THE EARTH THROUGH HER **VOLUNTEER WORK,** INCLUDING LAKE RESTORATION PROJECTS.

Hibah is an avionics engineer at NASA's Kennedy Space Center.

SUIT UP

How will new SPACE SUITS help us explore Mars?

Dig In

Will the astronauts heading to Mars have a closet full of space suits? It sounds like a crazy idea, but it's not as far-fetched as you might think. Picture your own closet: You have clothes for summer and others for winter, clothes you wear to school and uniforms for playing sports. Astronauts need different outfits for different activities, too. One of the coolest outfits, a next-generation space suit, will let astronauts explore the surface of Mars. Let's check it out.

What does a space suit do **?**

Why does it look so different from early space suits **?**

How do you put it on **?**

Life Preserver

We Earthlings are adapted for life on our planet—not in space or on Mars. We need an atmosphere that provides air to breathe and to shield us from the most extreme temperatures. The near-vacuum of space and Mars's thin, unwelcoming atmosphere don't provide that. So when we leave Earth, we must carry a little of its environment with us. Space suits, like spacecraft, do that for us. Since we're used to living in an atmosphere whose weight presses on us, space suits create air pressure to keep our body fluids in a liquid state. They also provide oxygen for us to breathe in, get rid of the carbon dioxide that we breathe out, and carry water to quench our thirst. They even include heating and cooling systems to keep us comfortable.

Bodyguard

It's not enough to support our life requirements. Space suits also have to protect us from the hazards of space, including radiation, dust storms, and space debris. They have to keep us safe on the planet's surface at all times—even if we trip on a rock and fall down! And if that's not enough, the space suits also must be flexible enough so we can move around.

How Things Worked

Since 1965, astronauts have left their spacecraft to go on space walks, walk on the moon, and work on satellites and space stations. For every one of those "EVAs" (extravehicular activities), they've had a space suit to protect them. The designs improved over the years and changed to meet new challenges. The first American space suits, worn by Mercury astronauts in the early 1960s, were based on the pressure suits worn by U.S. Navy pilots. They didn't have to provide much extra protection, because the Mercury astronauts stayed inside their spacecraft. That changed by the middle of the decade, when Gemini astronauts went on the first space walks. Their more advanced space suits still didn't include portable life-support systems. Instead, a cord ran from the suit to the life-support systems inside the Gemini spacecraft. That would not work for the Apollo astronauts, who explored the moon's surface in the late 1960s to the mid-1970s. To allow them to walk on the moon, the astronauts' space suits were changed to include boots that could handle a rocky surface and life-support systems worn on the astronauts' backs. Astronauts aboard the space shuttle, from the 1980s to the 1990s, and the International Space Station, from the 1990s to present, have multiple suits. They put on "extravehicular mobility units" to work outside the spacecraft for hours. The suits include life-support systems and jet packs. The Mars space suits will build on the best of these features to allow astronauts to explore the red planet.

helmet, gloves, and boots worn by the Mercury astronauts, 1961

Mercury 7 astronauts, 1959

extravehicular mobility unit

SUITED FOR MARS

Space suit engineers and designers are creating space suits that astronauts can wear to explore and work on the surface of Mars. They design, test, and redesign prototypes, like this cool-looking Z-2 prototype suit.

A bubble-shaped helmet visor provides a wider view of the astronaut's surroundings.

The upper torso is made of a hard composite material so it lasts a long time.

The Z-2 provides extra flexibility at joints so astronauts can move freely.

A portable life-support system provides oxygen and removes carbon dioxide.

Astronauts slip into the space suit from a hatch in the back—an idea designers borrowed from Russian space suits.

Glowing stripes will create better visibility in the dark.

Improved, integrated boots—similar to fancy hiking boots—will let astronauts walk stably on the rocky Martian surface.

NASA let the **PUBLIC VOTE** to pick the Z-2 space suit's design. The "technology" design, with its glowing stripes, beat out the shark-like "biomimicry" design and a sporty "trends in society" design.

FUN FACT

IT TAKES **MORE THAN 50** DIFFERENT TYPES OF PROFESSIONALS—INCLUDING ENGINEERS, SEAM SEWERS, MODEL MAKERS, AND TECHNICIANS—TO DESIGN AND **MAKE A SPACE SUIT.**

WANT TO KNOW MORE?

TELL ME MORE

"Space suit" is actually a bit misleading. It's not one suit; it's actually multiple pieces and layers. Beneath the cool-looking outer suit, astronauts wear special garments to provide cooling and ventilation. Other layers provide insulation or extra protection against hazards. Here's the tricky part. Even with all those layers, the suits need to be flexible enough for astronauts to move and work. To explore Mars, they need to be able to move their arms, hands, and legs freely so they can operate scientific gadgets, collect samples, build and repair equipment, and explore. Besides walking over rocks, up and down craters, and through Martian dust, they'll need to move in and out of rovers and base camp. It's a lot to ask of a suit, but designers have come up with a brilliant idea: The space suit may be able to latch on to the rover—kind of like how a spacecraft docks at the space station—so astronauts can slip out of the suit to move freely inside the rover and then slip back into the suit to explore outside.

Prototype Exploration Suit

FUN FACTS

● NASA also has designed and **built a prototype** space suit for using in low and microgravity, like on **space walks.** Called the Prototype Exploration Suit—or PXS, for short—it also may be modified for use on the **Martian surface.**

● **Designer fashion!** The Z-2 prototype space suit was designed by a **team of students** from Philadelphia University and NASA's own fashion designers.

TRY THIS!

Wonder what it feels like to wear a space suit? This experiment will give you a small taste of what it's like. Take a kitchen-size plastic garbage bag and put your bare arm inside. Wrap it snugly (not too tight) so it fits closely along the entire length of your arm. (A little tape might help keep it in place.) Now get active. Wave your arms, pump your fists, do jumping jacks, whatever—just keep the bag in place. After a couple of minutes, remove the bag. How did it feel inside there? A space suit is a bit like that plastic bag. It traps your body heat. After you took it off, your arm probably cooled down quickly. The warm air was released, and any sweat started to evaporate. Astronauts, of course, can't just yank off a sleeve! So NASA engineers had to get creative. They solved the heat problem with a liquid cooling and ventilation garment, which astronauts wear inside the space suit. This tight-fitting layer has little tubes that carry water to keep the astronauts comfortable. Cool idea—literally!

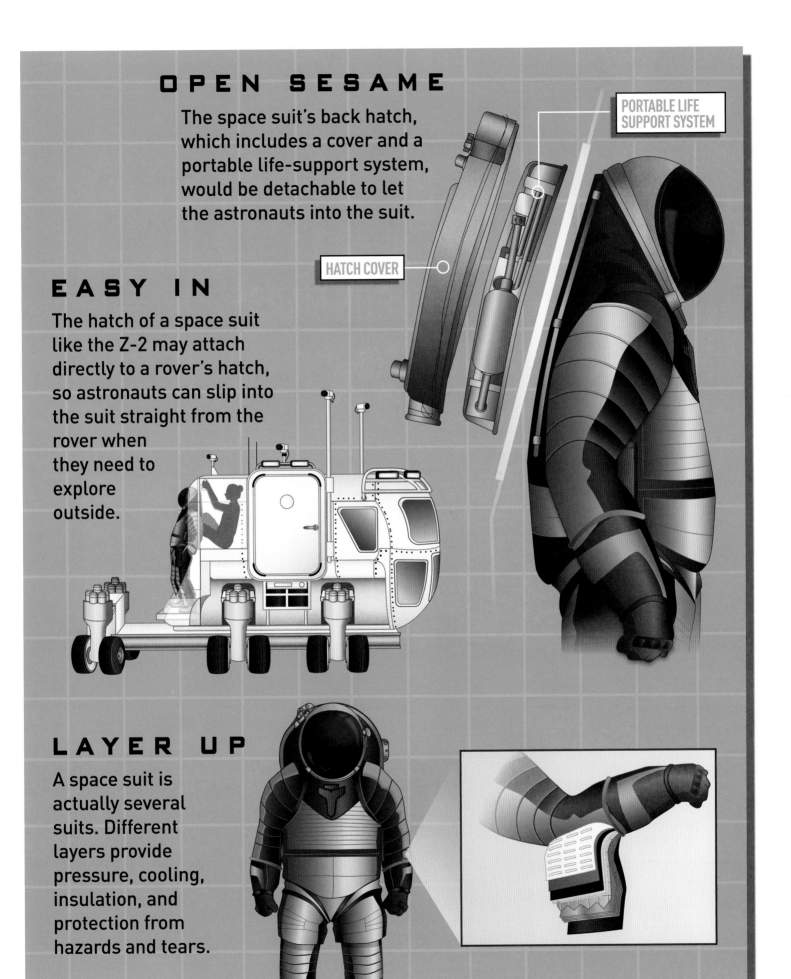

OPEN SESAME

The space suit's back hatch, which includes a cover and a portable life-support system, would be detachable to let the astronauts into the suit.

PORTABLE LIFE SUPPORT SYSTEM

HATCH COVER

EASY IN

The hatch of a space suit like the Z-2 may attach directly to a rover's hatch, so astronauts can slip into the suit straight from the rover when they need to explore outside.

LAYER UP

A space suit is actually several suits. Different layers provide pressure, cooling, insulation, and protection from hazards and tears.

LIVING OFF THE LAND

How can humans **LIVE ON MARS**?

Dig In

Pack your bags. We're heading to Mars. Well, maybe not this minute. But many scientists think we'll get there in the next couple of decades. Oh, sure, Mars is a dusty red planet with no breathable air, temperatures that plunge to minus 243 degrees Fahrenheit (-153 degrees Celsius), and no pizza. Details, details. We'll work it out! Read on to find out how we'd put a colony on the red planet.

Where will we live **?**

What will we eat **?**

How will we breathe **?**

Back to Basics

You have to look deeper than Mars's dusty red surface to see its potential as a home for humans. Think of what we humans need to live: food, water, shelter, and air. (Yes, you can live without TV and video games, if you really have to.) The red planet's surface and atmosphere are rich with resources that we can use to build habitats, grow food, and support life. We just need the technology to harvest those resources and convert them for our use—and scientists and engineers already are working on those solutions.

Advance Planning

Homes, work spaces, and greenhouses could be up and running before we humans even arrive. Robots would first be sent to the red planet to set up human habitats, such as the inflatable "Mars Ice Home," which would be insulated and have a shell filled with water to form an ice layer, shielding us from cosmic rays. Mars has lots of water—almost all of it just happens to be frozen. But equipment could extract water from the soil, which has ice mixed into it, or from underground layers. Other technology could suck in the Martian atmosphere and kick out oxygen for us to breathe. But what about dinner? At first, we'd bring a lot of dried food with us, but robots also could start growing veggies in greenhouses using hydroponic techniques, which use nutrient-rich liquid instead of soil, or even using the Martian soil. It'd be a while before pizza parlors dotted the Martian surface, but we wouldn't starve.

BUT ...

A lot of people—including brilliant scientists—are certain we could successfully colonize Mars. But should we? Some people raise a lot of objections: It would cost too much. We might pollute Mars like we did Earth. And, by the way, who gave us the right to transform another planet? But the pro-colony folks argue that humans might need a colony elsewhere in case something disastrous happens to Earth. Colonizing Mars also might help all humans unite as one people. Besides, it's in our very nature to be explorers. What do you think? Should we put a human colony on Mars?

FUN FACT

AT ITS CLOSEST APPROACH, MARS IS MORE THAN A **THOUSAND TIMES** FARTHER AWAY THAN OUR MOON. IT TOOK ASTRONAUTS THREE DAYS TO GET TO OUR MOON BACK IN THE 1960s. **IT'LL TAKE ABOUT SIX MONTHS** TO REACH MARS.

HOME, SWEET HOME

It would be too hard to bring everything a colony needs from Earth. The first humans on Mars would bring along some lightweight materials and technology, but they also would use as many of the red planet's resources as possible to create a colony.

Homes and work spaces could be linked together in a **MODULAR** fashion to allow us to get from one place to another without having to put on space suits. The habitats would protect us from Mars's bitter cold temperatures, lack of breathable air, and radiation.

Enclosed, pressurized **ROVERS** would let us move around the planet quickly and allow us to take off our helmets inside to be more comfortable. They could be docked with habitat modules.

GREENHOUSES and hydroponics bays, which use nutrient-rich solutions to grow plants, would provide fresh veggies. The Martian soil already has at least some of the nutrients plants need.

Insulated, **INFLATABLE BUILDINGS,** such as the "Mars Ice Home," shaped like a fat donut with a teeny hole and surrounded by an ice shell, would go up fast and could be some of the first dwellings and work spaces. Some parts could be 3D-printed using materials extracted from Mars, and the layer of ice would shield us from radiation.

Large **SOLAR PANELS** could capture the sun's rays to power the colony.

Some permanent habitats could be **UNDERGROUND,** in Martian caves or tunnel-like lava tubes, to protect us from radiation, which otherwise would damage our body's cells. They also could be formed from inflatable modules.

The planet Mars is named after the **ROMAN GOD OF WAR.** Its red color—caused by rusted iron in its dusty surface—reminded early astronomers of blood. But it's actually a pretty peaceful place.

FUN FACT

NASA WANTS TO LAND PEOPLE ON THE RED PLANET IN THE **2030s.** BUT THE SPACE AGENCY HAS COMPETITION, INCLUDING ELON MUSK AND HIS **SpaceX ROCKETS** AND CARGO CARRIERS.

WANT TO KNOW MORE?

TELL ME MORE

A GREENER RED PLANET?

Bitter cold temperatures. No air to breathe. Killer radiation. Sounds inviting, doesn't it? If only Mars could be more like Earth! Well, maybe it can. A recent scientific study suggested that Mars actually was similar to Earth a mere four billion years ago, maybe with rippling oceans and lakes, flowing rivers, and blue skies with billowy white clouds. But then its atmosphere started drifting off into space, transforming Mars into a cold, barren wasteland. Now its atmosphere is 100 times thinner than Earth's—way too thin to protect us from the sun's harmful ultraviolet rays, insulate us from the extreme cold, or maintain a nice atmospheric pressure. But scientists are working on ways to restore a thicker, protective atmosphere that eventually may even have enough oxygen for us to breathe.

WARMING UP

Mars's atmosphere is blown away by solar wind, a stream of electrically charged particles that break free from the sun's outer layer and zoom out in all directions. But scientists think it may be possible to shield Mars from some of the solar wind by creating a nearby magnetic field. The magnetic shield would let the old Martian atmosphere rebuild itself. Slightly warmer temperatures would trigger a greenhouse effect, releasing carbon dioxide (CO_2)—a gas that traps heat—from Mars's frozen polar caps. On Earth, greenhouse gases are a problem, but on Mars, they'd help create a better environment for life by filling the thin atmosphere and heating the planet. Eventually, warmer weather could melt the ice and restore the oceans. Scientists aren't sure exactly how long it would take, but they believe the shield would speed up efforts to transform the Martian environment into one more like Earth's, a process called terraforming. Without the shield, terraforming could take hundreds of years—maybe even a thousand!

Whoa ... SLOW DOWN! A Closer Look at Magnetospheres

Why all the excitement about magnetic shields? Well, we wouldn't be able to breathe without them! Earth's atmosphere is held in place by a giant magnetic bubble called the magnetosphere. It's kind of like a force field shielding our atmosphere from that pesky solar wind that'd be all too happy to blow it away. Earth's magnetosphere is natural, and it's one of the strongest of all the rocky planets' in our solar system. It's like a protective cushion, insulating us from getting too hot or cold, shielding us from a lot of the sun's harmful ultraviolet rays, and maintaining a nice atmospheric pressure for us. Earth's magnetosphere is generated in the planet's deep interior by fluid material that conducts electricity. The magnetic energy is conducted along a line from one pole to another. It's what makes our compass needles point north! Mars used to have a natural magnetic field, and scientists are trying to figure out what happened to it—and maybe to restore it. In the meantime, if you travel to Mars, don't bother bringing your compass. It wouldn't work.

TRY THIS!

Do you feel the air pressing down on you? You don't? Well, it does—you're just used to the feeling. Earth's atmosphere is constantly putting almost 15 pounds of pressure per square inch (1.1 kg/sq cm) on us (at sea level). It's a pretty powerful force, and we're always pushing out against it. To get a sense of how strong that force is, try this simple experiment (over a sink). Fill a cup one-third with water. Cover the entire rim with an index card, and hold the card in place.

Turn the cup upside down, and take your hand off the index card. If everything worked right, those 15 pounds of air pressure pushing up will hold the card in place. The little bit of water pushing down exerts much less force. The pressure that air exerts on us depends where we are. With its really thin atmosphere, Mars exerts hardly any atmospheric pressure—and that's not good for us Earthlings. We'd have to wear pressure suits to live on Mars, just like we do in the near-vacuum of space.

TRANSFORMATION

We could live on Mars now—as long as we're bundled in protective space suits. To live and work outside, we'd need a protective atmosphere with air to breathe. To get it, we'd have to transform the red planet into a much greener and bluer version, more similar to Earth, a process called terraforming.

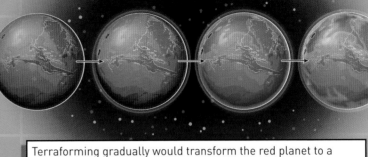

Terraforming gradually would transform the red planet to a more Earthlike environment. It would create a warmer environment and atmosphere, and ice would melt to restore oceans.

PLANETARY PROTECTOR

The magnetic shield would be "parked" in space at an orbit where the gravitational pulls from Mars and the sun are balanced.

MARS

The shield would use a closed electric circuit powerful enough to create a magnetic field.

The magnet would create a shield that would block the solar wind, preventing it from blowing away the renewed Martian atmosphere.

If we can get Mars to rebuild its atmosphere, what's going to keep the solar wind from blowing it away again? Some scientists have an interesting idea. They've proposed putting an inflatable structure, which would create a protective magnetic shield, into orbit between Mars and the sun.

FUN FACTS

● NASA has been studying Mars for more than **40 years** using unmanned spacecraft and rovers.

● Gravity, the force that holds us down on our planet, is much different on Mars. It's only about **one-third the strength** of Earth's gravity. That means buildings don't have to be as strong to handle the force. And you can jump **way higher!**

TALES FROM THE LAB

IS ANYONE OUT THERE?

SEARCHING FOR EXTRATERRESTRIAL LIFE

Do you believe that life exists elsewhere in the universe?

It's a question we Earthlings have pondered for most of our existence. The universe is vast. If it exists, where do we look for extraterrestrial life?

LISTEN UP!

In 1959, physicists Giuseppe Cocconi and Philip Morrison figured that our best hope was that intelligent life had evolved elsewhere, had better technology than ours, and would contact us. They'd probably send a message on a light-speed electromagnetic wave. But to receive it, we'd need to tune in to the correct frequency, like a radio station. How would we know which one?

66 WHERE DO WE LOOK FOR EXTRATERRESTRIAL LIFE? 99

Hmm, what would Earthlings and E.T.'s have in common? Hydrogen! It's the most common element in the universe and, like all elements, emits an electromagnetic frequency. Soon, scientists around the world tuned in to hydrogen's frequency. They built high-tech facilities, like the SETI (Search for Extraterrestrial Intelligence) Institute, to scan for signals.

But then they had another idea: Why just listen?

"HI, MY NAME'S EARTH"

We decided to send out messages of our own.

Astronomers Frank Drake and Carl Sagan convinced NASA to put a greeting on board the Pioneer 10 and 11 spacecraft launched in 1972 and 1973. The greeting was an etched plaque depicting a man (waving—to show we're friendly), a woman, and maps of our solar system. Come visit!

Voyager 1 and 2, launched in 1977, carried gold-plated discs telling about Earth and human civilization. They included images, greetings, music, maps, and nature sounds from all over the world. A diagram of hydrogen provided a key to decoding the messages.

But the chances that the spacecraft would bump into intelligent life on their journeys? With space as big and vast as it is, the probability that one spacecraft moving in one direction could make contact is pretty unlikely. Scientists realized they needed to refine their search.

WHERE ARE YOU?

Where would extraterrestrial life exist?

Just a few decades ago, we only knew about nine planets—those orbiting our sun (including Pluto at the time). But in 1995, scientists discovered a planet orbiting a star like our sun. Our solar system wasn't unique! Since then, scientists have confirmed more than 3,000 planets, with the possibility of thousands more.

Could one of them support life? Which one?

Scientists search for planets that have liquid water—a key condition for life as we know it. To find them, astronomers look first at how closely planets orbit their stars. If they're too close, any water would boil and evaporate; if too far, water would freeze.

But planets also need the right climate to support water and life. Since we can't travel (yet) to distant planets, astrobiologists, like Aomawa Shields, learn about their climates by taking what we already know—the planets' size, mass, orbits—and using computer models to fill in the blanks.

They've already identified several good prospects and will study them more closely for signs of life. The life may only be single-celled microbes, and it may not even appear in a form of life we're already familiar with. But scientists aren't ruling out the chance of finding intelligent life somewhere someday.

Our galaxy has hundreds of billions of stars—almost every one with a planet—and there are hundreds of billions of galaxies, Aomawa Shields points out. "The odds of our planet being the only planet on which life has developed, emerged, evolved? Pretty low."

BY THE MID-2020s, THREE NEW HUGE GROUND-BASED TELESCOPES SHOULD "SEE FIRST LIGHT" OR START LOOKING INTO SPACE. FOR STARGAZERS, THEIR NAMES AREN'T THE MOST INSPIRED: THE EUROPEAN EXTREMELY LARGE TELESCOPE, THE GIANT MAGELLAN TELESCOPE, AND THE THIRTY METER TELESCOPE.

Deep Space Station 43, an antenna that enables communication with faraway missions

James Webb Space Telescope

Kepler–62f, a planet far from Earth

the Pioneer 10 satellite, orbiting Jupiter

Make It BETTER!

Imagine having to come up with a way to introduce Earth and human civilization to intelligent extraterrestrials. What would you say? How would you say it? You would have no idea how the aliens communicated. Would they use words? Symbols? Math? Gestures? All of the above?

That was the challenge confronting Carl Sagan and Frank Drake when they designed the Pioneer plaque. They only had a few weeks to come up with an idea—and a lot of people think they blew it. People criticized the design for all sorts of reasons: some symbols were confusing, the people didn't represent all humans, and—*gasp*—they were naked! So when NASA prepared to send Voyager 1 and 2 out in 1977, they spent more time working on the message, making sure that it represented many different cultures and the diversity of Earth.

Do you think they got it right the second time? What would you change? How would you try to communicate with intelligent life far out in the universe?

AOMAWA SHIELDS IS NOT JUST AN ASTRONOMER; SHE'S A CLASSICALLY **TRAINED ACTOR!** SHE USED TO WORK IN HOLLYWOOD.

THE IDEA OF ALIENS BEING **"LITTLE GREEN MEN"** MAY BE TRACED BACK AS FAR AS A FOLKTALE FROM THE 12TH CENTURY ABOUT MYSTERIOUS GREEN CHILDREN.

ARE WE THERE YET?

How could DEEP SLEEP ease our journey into deep space?

Dig In

You know how it goes. You're leaving on an awesome trip, and you're so excited that you could burst. But first, there's the long, very long, really long, excruciatingly long ride to get there. Hours locked in a car? *Noooo!* So how'd you like to travel six months or more to Mars? (Shhh. We can hear you scream.) Take a deep breath. Researchers think they have a solution: Let travelers hibernate on the way. Read on to see how it'd work.

What happens when you hibernate **?**

How would we wake up **?**

Wouldn't we get hungry **?**

JUST THE FACTS

Be the Bear

One of the challenges of getting to Mars is handling the six-month (or longer) trip to reach the red planet. Researchers are working on ways to let us sleep most of the way. Not normal sleep, but a really deep sleep—like hibernation, in which our body's functions would slow down and we wouldn't really be aware of what's going on. It would slash the costs of the journey, because we wouldn't have to pack as much food, water, oxygen, and other supplies. And it'd keep us from going bonkers from boredom. Win-win.

SUPER SLEEPERS

It may be unusual for humans to hibernate, but it's routine for some other mammals. Check out how these **super sleepers** catch some z's.

Black bear: This carnivore hibernates three to five months out of a year. To prepare for the long period, it eats a lot—gaining up to 30 pounds (13.6 kg) a week.

Groundhog: This rodent's heart rate slows to only about five beats per minute during its hibernation, which can last up to six months—or at least until it's roused to predict spring's arrival!

Prairie dog: During its four- to five-month hibernation, this rodent wakes up to eat on warmer days.

Fat-tail dwarf lemur: One of a few primates—our closest relatives—known to hibernate, the dwarf lemur gorges on fruit, insects, and flowers during Madagascar's short rainy season and stores fat in its tail so it can hibernate up to seven months during droughts.

SNORE CITY

We're far from having a hibernation plan in place for deep-space travel—and it may not be the way we travel to Mars after all. But researchers are working on plans just in case. One idea shows how a spacecraft could haul a hundred hibernating passengers to Mars.

Each habitat would have a docking hatch to attach to another module in the spacecraft, so the crew could move the entire length of the spacecraft.

Large modules would carry 48 passengers each.

The spacecraft's crew would have their own module. Crew members would take turns hibernating, so four crew members would be awake the entire trip.

BEDROOM

The 48 passengers in each habitat module would be divided into multiple levels. They wouldn't need room to run around, so their sleep pods could be close together, saving space and resources for the spacecraft.

Since we humans don't usually hibernate, it'd take some advanced technology to put us into torpor, a sleepy state where our bodies and brains wouldn't be as active. Our body's temperature would gradually be lowered to about 89 to 93 degrees Fahrenheit (32 to 34 degrees Celsius) over about six hours. That temperature drop would slow down our metabolism—all the processes in our bodies that work together to create the energy that keeps us going. We wouldn't need as much nutrition to stay alive. And we definitely wouldn't get bored!

The REAL DEAL

The idea of putting space travelers into deep sleep is nothing new. Science fiction has used the technique for decades! But how close are science-fiction stories to science fact? In both fiction and fact, deep sleep requires dropping a space traveler's body temperature and using advanced pods to care for the hibernating travelers. The researchers studying human hibernation even used photos from sci-fi movies when they presented their ideas! But some fictional stories have taken the temperature drop too far—and that has created a misunderstanding among the public. Many people think deep-space travel would use cryogenic technology, in which people would be completely frozen and then slowly warmed back up. Cryogenic techniques have worked with very small tissue samples, and researchers are trying to improve them. But entire humans? No way. That's just fiction (at least for now).

SLEEPY TIME

Putting space travelers in a state of hibernation would decrease their need for food, room, and entertainment—making it easier to transport them into deep space.

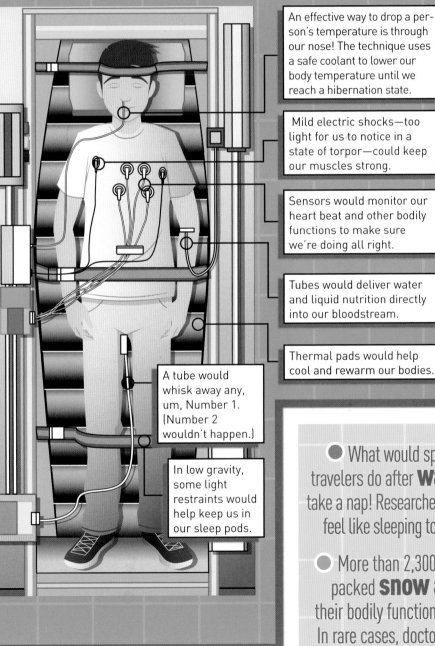

An effective way to drop a person's temperature is through our nose! The technique uses a safe coolant to lower our body temperature until we reach a hibernation state.

Mild electric shocks—too light for us to notice in a state of torpor—could keep our muscles strong.

Sensors would monitor our heart beat and other bodily functions to make sure we're doing all right.

Tubes would deliver water and liquid nutrition directly into our bloodstream.

Thermal pads would help cool and rewarm our bodies.

A tube would whisk away any, um, Number 1. (Number 2 wouldn't happen.)

In low gravity, some light restraints would help keep us in our sleep pods.

FUN FACTS

● What would space travelers do after **waking up** from hibernation? Probably take a nap! Researchers believe that **hibernating** wouldn't feel like sleeping to people, so we'd actually wake up tired.

○ More than 2,300 years ago, Greek physician Hippocrates packed **snow and ice** into soldiers' wounds to slow their bodily functions, giving them more **time to heal.** In rare cases, doctors today also **lower a patient's body temperature** for a short period to get more time for life-saving medical and surgical care.

SIDEKICK

How does **ROBONAUT** help space exploration?

Dig In

Imagine what you could do with a robot helper. If a jar of peanut butter is hard to open, have your robot lend a hand. Boring chores? No more! Your robot could do them—and it wouldn't even complain. And it would hang out with you whenever you wanted. No surprise, then, that astronauts have a cool robot companion to help them on the International Space Station. Come meet Robonaut 2—and, yes, it goes by "R2." Coincidence? We think not.

What does Robonaut 2 do?

Can it think for itself?

How does it move around?

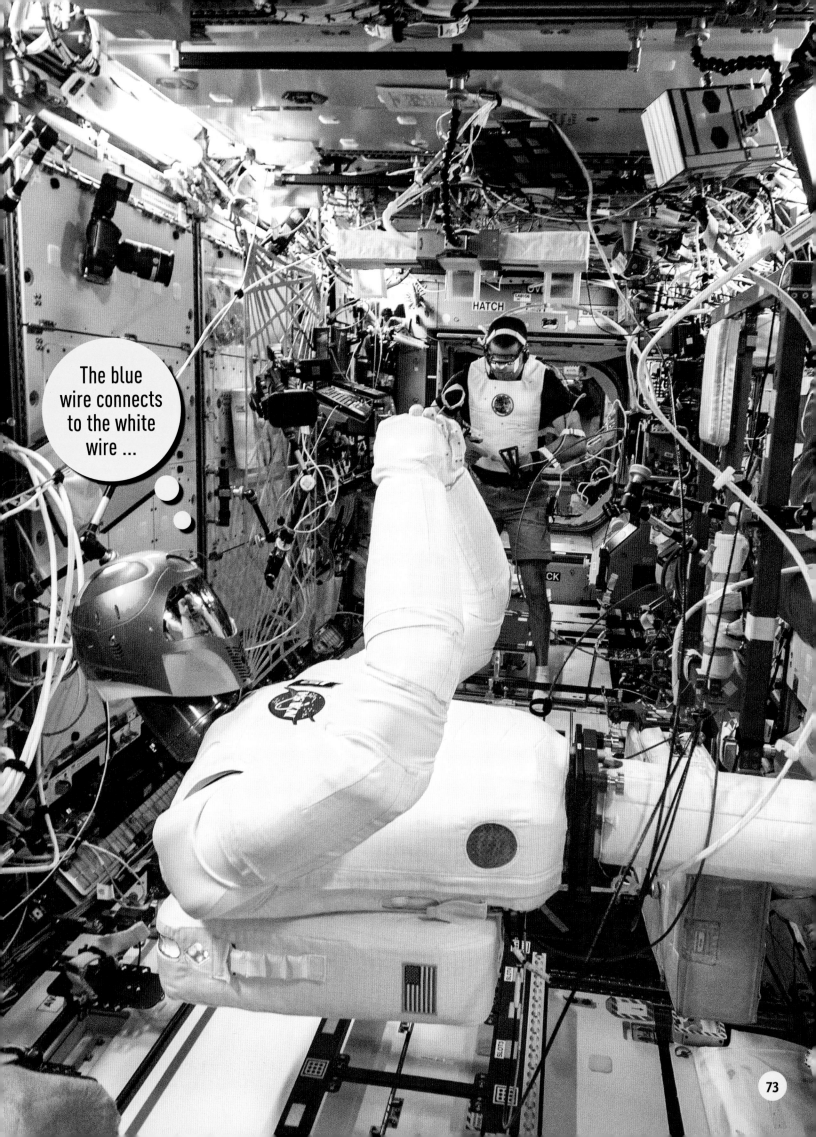

JUST THE FACTS

Astronaut's Aide

Robonaut 2 is not the first robot in space. That honor goes to the robotic probes and rovers that have explored space and planets for half a century. But R2 is the first humanoid robot in space, one designed to look like a person—and act a bit like one, too. It's easier for a humanoid robot to do the same jobs as an astronaut. NASA hopes R2 can take over some of the routine tasks on board the space station, such as setting up tools and equipment, so the astronauts can work on more challenging parts of the mission. Astronauts or NASA operators can assign R2 a task and let it draw on its programming to figure out how to do it. Or they can take over R2's controls, seeing through its camera eyes, and control how it moves—like a really advanced puppet.

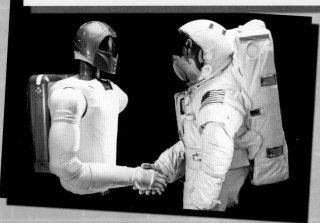

Moving Up

Though R2 arrived on the space station in 2011, it didn't get legs for another three years. Unlike the rest of its body, the legs are more spidery than human, but that makes it more versatile on the space station. If R2 passes all its tests on board the station, it may get to take a space walk so scientists can learn how it handles open space. They hope it eventually can help maintain and repair the space station on the outside.

ROBOTS OF THE FUTURE?

We humans have been fascinated with robots for **nearly a century**—but reality didn't keep up with our imaginations. Take a look at how shows and magazines of the past presented **our future with robots.**

1951: Gort, a character in the film *The Day the Earth Stood Still*, travels to Earth from a distant planet and acts as a type of interstellar police officer. He maintains the peace by vaporizing weapons with a laser he shoots from his head.

1956: Robby the Robot appears in the movie *Forbidden Planet*. Intelligent and friendly, he helps a crew of Earthlings contact home after they land on a distant planet. Robby becomes a science-fiction star, appearing in television shows for years.

1958: *Popular Electronics* imagines robots being such a central part of our lives, they'd be like members of our families. They'd even celebrate holidays with us.

1962: Strong, no-nonsense Rosie takes care of the household for the Jetsons and even steps in to parent at times.

1968: The Russian magazine *Ogoniok* ("Little Flame") makes us imagine a time when strong, friendly robots befriend and look after kids.

FUN FACT

THE TERM "ROBOT" WAS INTRODUCED IN 1920 BY CZECH WRITER KAREL ČAPEK IN HIS HIT PLAY, *R.U.R.* (ROSSUM'S UNIVERSAL ROBOTS). THE WORD IS DRAWN FROM AN OLD CHURCH **SLAVONIC WORD,** *ROBOTA*, WHICH MEANS "FORCED LABOR" OR "SERVITUDE."

SHIP'S MATE

Robonaut 2, the first humanoid robot in space, is designed to take over boring or dangerous jobs, so astronauts can focus on other work.

It "sees" using cameras inside its head. Astronauts also can view what the cameras record on a separate display.

R2's flexible neck allows it to look up and down and from side to side.

R2's legs are more like an extra pair of arms. Human-like legs would be useless in microgravity, where astronauts float instead of walk.

In place of feet, it has clamps that let it latch onto things and climb around.

R2 can either be plugged into a power source or wear a battery pack on its back.

Computer processors in the torso run the robot's programs. Yes, R2 thinks with its stomach!

Each arm is about two feet eight inches (81 cm) long for a total wingspan of eight feet (2.4 m).

The hands and fingers move like a human's so it can perform similar tasks.

You may want to grow bigger, but **BETTER TECHNOLOGY** helps robots get smaller. Robonaut 2 is 3 feet 4 inches tall (1 m) from its waist to its head, and it weighs 330 pounds (150 kg). The first Robonaut was almost twice as tall and 80 pounds (36 kg) heavier.

FUN FACT

GOOD THING ROBONAUT 2 CAN **SHAKE HANDS.** IT RECEIVED A LOT OF CONGRATULATIONS FOR WINNING NASA'S GOVERNMENT **INVENTION OF THE YEAR** IN 2014.

WANT TO KNOW MORE?

TELL ME MORE

THE RIGHT TOUCH

Don't think of the robots and droids you've seen in your favorite movies. This R2 doesn't take matters into its own hands—or give snippy responses. But it still can do amazing things. It's packed with hundreds of sensors and advanced technology, which it uses to detect its surroundings and maneuver around. Its visual system is so advanced that it can "see" depth and movement. Most impressive are its hands, which can grip things precisely—either with a delicate touch or a strong hold. R2 is handy to have around—literally.

ON A ROLL
R2's torso can be detached from its legs and mounted on a wheeled vehicle, which may be better for exploring the surfaces of planets and moons.

FUN FACTS

● NASA wants to send a humanoid robot—if not Robonaut, then some other—to asteroids and eventually to **Mars** and Mars's moons to serve as a scout, map the sites, and **prepare structures for later human explorers.**

● R2 has a modular construction. Astronauts can assemble its body **piece by piece.**

● Many of the technologies developed for **Robonaut** may help right here on Earth. The Robo-Glove, which **increases the strength of a human's grasp,** could help factory workers. A robotic exoskeleton based on Robonaut technology could help people with limited mobility walk.

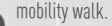

The REAL DEAL

Is Robonaut 2 intelligent? You may have heard of "artificial intelligence," computers or robots that think in ways like humans do—learning from experience, making generalizations, reasoning. Some people don't think R2 meets that definition because it's programmed to perform tasks. When an astronaut or NASA controller assigns it a job, it must draw on its programming to complete the work. But don't we all draw on our training? Some people believe that when robots react to things they see or hear, they're showing a type of humanlike intelligence. R2 uses its sensors to gather information about its environment, and it uses that to follow instructions to do its work. What do you think? Is R2 intelligent?

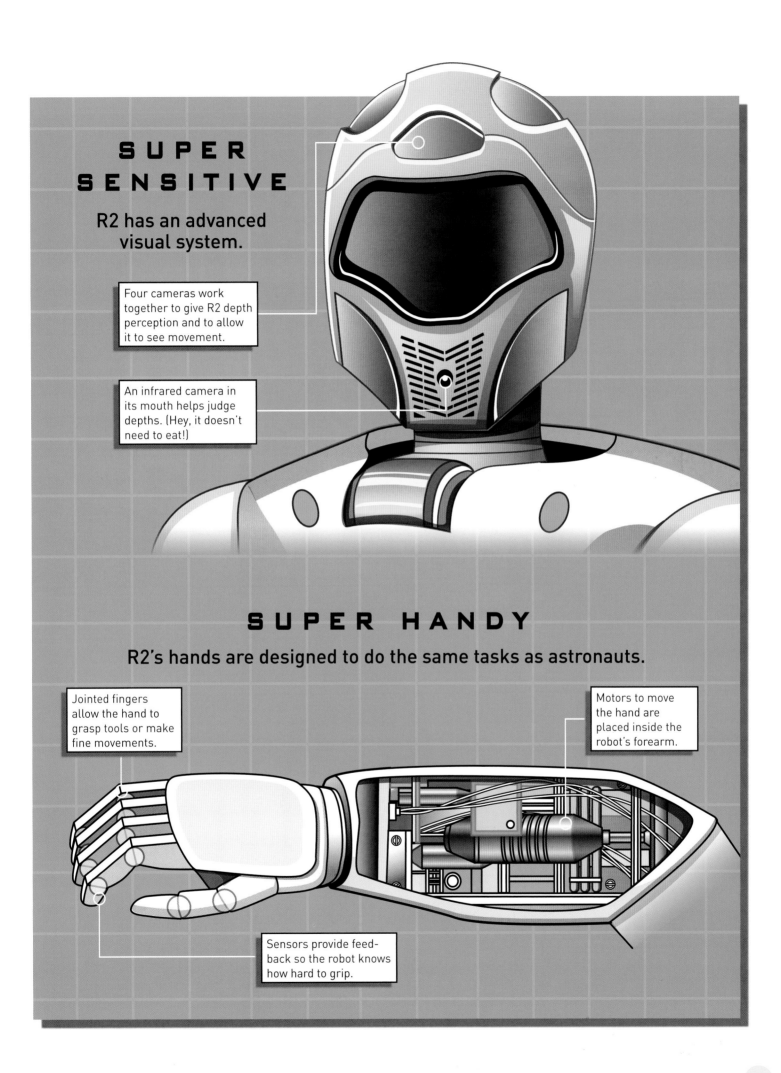

SUPER SENSITIVE

R2 has an advanced visual system.

Four cameras work together to give R2 depth perception and to allow it to see movement.

An infrared camera in its mouth helps judge depths. (Hey, it doesn't need to eat!)

SUPER HANDY

R2's hands are designed to do the same tasks as astronauts.

Jointed fingers allow the hand to grasp tools or make fine movements.

Motors to move the hand are placed inside the robot's forearm.

Sensors provide feed-back so the robot knows how hard to grip.

TRY THIS!

SPIN CONTROL

MAKE AND PLAY A ROCKET-LAUNCH GAME

The Earth spins at about 1,000 miles an hour (1,609 km/h). And, of course, it orbits the sun—as do the other planets in our solar system. That's a lot of spinning and circling—and it adds an extra challenge to launching rockets from Earth toward Mars. It's already going to take six months or more to get there. You want to make sure you blast off when your rocket is pointing the right way! This game will give you a little taste of how challenging that can be.

WHAT TO DO

1. YOU NEED YOUR LAZY SUSAN to be flat on top. If it isn't, cut out a circle from your poster board or cardboard that's a little bigger than the Lazy Susan and tape it on top. (Trick it out with decorations, if you want.)

2. SPACE OUT YOUR TARGETS (baskets, shoe boxes, whatever) on the ground. Use as many as you want. (You can make the game harder by using fewer targets.)

3. STEP BACK A LITTLE from the targets and roll your balls toward them. See how close you can get to the targets. (You won't be using the Lazy Susan yet.)

4. NOW PUT THE LAZY SUSAN between you and the targets.

5. GIVE THE LAZY SUSAN a good spin. Roll your balls across the top of the Lazy Susan toward the targets, and see how close you can get to them now.

ALTERNATIVE: This game is also fun to play if you can find a playground with a merry-go-round (the kind you push and ride, not the kind with horses). Try to toss the balls into baskets as you're riding around, and compare that to how you do when you're standing still. This is a great game to play with friends, too.

WHAT TO EXPECT

IT'S NOT IMPOSSIBLE TO HIT TARGETS WHEN YOU ROLL BALLS ACROSS A SPINNING CIRCLE—BUT IT SURE IS A LOT HARDER!

WHAT'S GOING ON?

JUST LIKE THE LAZY SUSAN OR MERRY-GO-ROUND, THE EARTH'S MOTION PRESENTS AN EXTRA CHALLENGE WHEN LAUNCHING A ROCKET. SPACE SCIENTISTS AND ENGINEERS MUST TIME A ROCKET LAUNCH SO THE EARTH'S MOTION HELPS (DOESN'T HURT) ITS FLIGHT. THEY EVEN USE THE EARTH'S MOTION TO GIVE A BOOST TO THE ROCKET. THEY AIM THE ROCKET SO IT TRAVELS THE SAME DIRECTION AS THE EARTH'S ORBIT, AND THEY POINT IT A BIT TO THE EAST TO TAKE ADVANTAGE OF THE EARTH'S EASTWARD ROTATION. NOW THAT'S A BIG LAUNCHPAD!

IT'S A LOT TO THINK ABOUT: THE ORBITS, THE SPINNING, THE TIME OF YEAR. SPACE ENGINEERS AND SCIENTISTS LOOK AT ALL THAT INFORMATION TO PICK THE BEST DAYS FOR A ROCKET LAUNCH, THE "LAUNCH WINDOW." THEY USUALLY SCHEDULE A LAUNCH EARLY IN THE WINDOW. THAT WAY, IF THE WEATHER'S BAD OR SOMETHING GOES WRONG, THEY'LL STILL HAVE TIME FOR ANOTHER SHOT.

CHAPTER 3

OUR CRAZY PLANET

YOU DON'T NEED TO JET INTO SPACE TO SEE OTHERWORLDLY SIGHTS.

Good old planet Earth has plenty to offer. Cosmic light shows, bizarre rock formations, lakes and mountains in freaky colors, stones that mysteriously move, geysers that blast water into the sky. And speaking of the sky, watch out for the fury of tornadoes and hurricanes! It's never a dull moment on our crazy planet!

SPOUTING OFF

How do GEYSERS blast boiling hot water and steam into the sky?

Dig In

When geysers lose their cool, there's no mistaking it. They erupt in streams of scalding water and steam. Some shoot straight up, while others burble close to the ground. But make no mistake about it, these rare geologic features are no ordinary water fountains! Let's find out what gets a geyser so steamed.

Why is the water so hot?

Why are geysers different shapes?

How often do they erupt?

It can take **500 YEARS** for water to seep from the surface to a geyser's reservoir. When a geyser erupts, we might be seeing water **OLDER** than the **U.S.A.!**

Master Blasters

Geysers are some of the most amazing and bizarre geologic phenomena in the world. They erupt like volcanoes, but instead of shooting molten rock into the sky, geysers send up a jet of boiling-hot water and steam. Some geysers erupt on a fairly regular schedule—whether minutes, hours, or days—but most are pretty unpredictable. And while typical eruptions last a few seconds or minutes, a few geysers can blast water for an hour!

Rare Finds

Geysers are extremely rare. A type of hot spring, they only exist in places where specific ingredients come together: lots of underground water, hot rocks to heat it, and a vent to the ground's surface. Underground, the hot rocks superheat the trapped groundwater. It builds up so much pressure that it finally blasts its way up the vent to the surface.

GREAT GUSHERS

Geysers come in **all shapes and sizes**, and some erupt regularly while others are unpredictable. Here are some **standouts.**

The famous **Old Faithful**, in Yellowstone National Park, U.S.A., gets its name from its eruptions occurring about every 60 to 90 minutes, some 100 to 200 feet (30 to 60 m) into the air.

Strokkur, Iceland's most famous geyser, erupts every four to 20 minutes, shooting water up to 100 feet (30 m). It's an amazing height for a wide-based fountain geyser.

El Tatio (The Grandfather) is a field of geysers nestled in the Andes Mountains in northern Chile. At 13,780 feet (4,200 m) above sea level, it's one of the world's highest geyser fields.

Velikan ("Giant") is one of the stars of the Valley of Geysers (Dolina geiserov) on Russia's Kamchatka Peninsula, the second largest concentration of geysers in the world after Yellowstone. Velikan erupts every five to seven hours, sending water 115 feet (35 m) into the air.

Steamboat Geyser, in Yellowstone, is the world's tallest, shooting water more than 300 feet (91 m) into the air. But you have to be lucky to see it. It's unpredictable and infrequent—sometimes erupting after several days, sometimes after half a century—and some of its eruptions only reach 40 feet (12 m).

Castle Geyser, which is close to Old Faithful in Yellowstone, is probably the oldest geyser in the world. Its cone—the largest in Yellowstone—is estimated to be between 5,000 and 15,000 years old. It erupts every 10 to 12 hours for as long as an hour. Its cone shape reminds people of a castle.

Andernach Geyser, in Germany, is the world's tallest cold-water geyser. Yes, cold water! Its pressurized water is not driven up by steam but by dissolved carbon dioxide—like a shaken bottle of soda.

THAR SHE BLOWS!

Geysers occur only in places where several unusual geologic features come together.

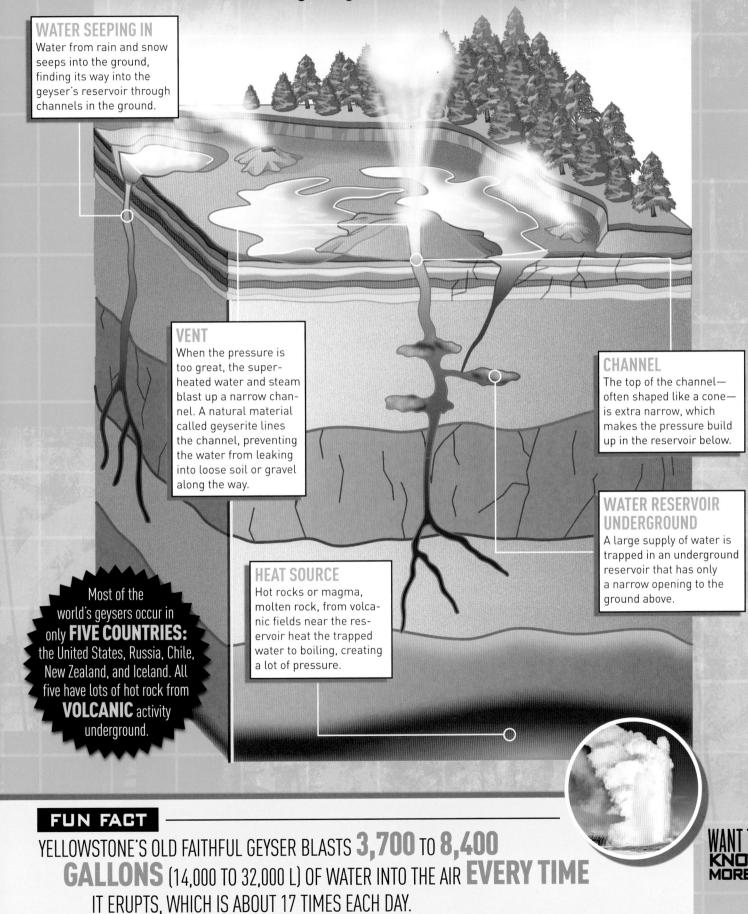

WATER SEEPING IN
Water from rain and snow seeps into the ground, finding its way into the geyser's reservoir through channels in the ground.

VENT
When the pressure is too great, the super-heated water and steam blast up a narrow channel. A natural material called geyserite lines the channel, preventing the water from leaking into loose soil or gravel along the way.

CHANNEL
The top of the channel—often shaped like a cone—is extra narrow, which makes the pressure build up in the reservoir below.

WATER RESERVOIR UNDERGROUND
A large supply of water is trapped in an underground reservoir that has only a narrow opening to the ground above.

HEAT SOURCE
Hot rocks or magma, molten rock, from volcanic fields near the reservoir heat the trapped water to boiling, creating a lot of pressure.

Most of the world's geysers occur in only **FIVE COUNTRIES:** the United States, Russia, Chile, New Zealand, and Iceland. All five have lots of hot rock from **VOLCANIC** activity underground.

FUN FACT

YELLOWSTONE'S OLD FAITHFUL GEYSER BLASTS **3,700** TO **8,400** **GALLONS** (14,000 TO 32,000 L) OF WATER INTO THE AIR **EVERY TIME** IT ERUPTS, WHICH IS ABOUT 17 TIMES EACH DAY.

WANT TO KNOW MORE?

TELL ME MORE

Even when you have all the ingredients for a geyser—underground water, hot rocks, a vent—they come together in different configurations to produce various shapes and sizes. Some geysers blast thousands of gallons (or liters) high up in the air, but others burble up in a shorter, bushy shape. If you take away any of the ingredients, you end up with different, but still awesome, geologic phenomena, such as fumaroles, mud pots, and simple hot springs. There are even some geysers in the depths of the ocean!

WHOA ... SLOW DOWN! A Closer Look at Steam

To really understand how a geyser works, you need to remember what happens when water turns into steam. To become steam, water must be heated to its boiling point. As it goes from liquid to gas, it expands a lot. If we could watch the microscopic particles inside it during that change, we'd see them moving around, bumping into and bouncing off each other. As they heat up in the gas, they fly around faster and faster, needing much more room. When the boiling happens in a confined space, like a geyser's underground reservoir, the expanded gas has nowhere to go (at least for a while). It gets squeezed together, building up a lot of pressure. Eventually, it becomes too much to contain—the steam needs somewhere to go, so it blasts the water out of the vent.

SPURTS, SQUIRTS, AND BURBLES

A few tweaks in geologic conditions can create really different phenomena. Not only do geysers come in different shapes, but they have some amazing hot spring cousins.

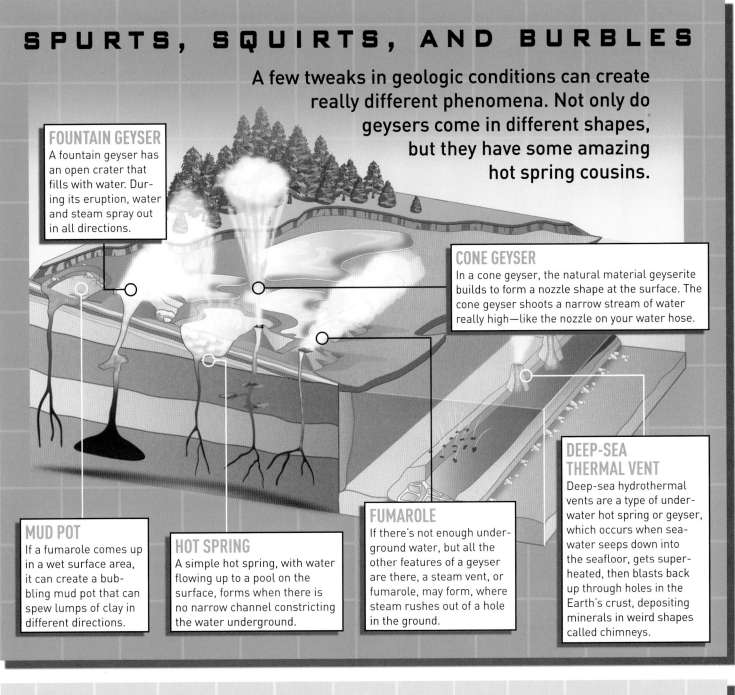

FOUNTAIN GEYSER
A fountain geyser has an open crater that fills with water. During its eruption, water and steam spray out in all directions.

CONE GEYSER
In a cone geyser, the natural material geyserite builds to form a nozzle shape at the surface. The cone geyser shoots a narrow stream of water really high—like the nozzle on your water hose.

DEEP-SEA THERMAL VENT
Deep-sea hydrothermal vents are a type of underwater hot spring or geyser, which occurs when seawater seeps down into the seafloor, gets superheated, then blasts back up through holes in the Earth's crust, depositing minerals in weird shapes called chimneys.

FUMAROLE
If there's not enough underground water, but all the other features of a geyser are there, a steam vent, or fumarole, may form, where steam rushes out of a hole in the ground.

MUD POT
If a fumarole comes up in a wet surface area, it can create a bubbling mud pot that can spew lumps of clay in different directions.

HOT SPRING
A simple hot spring, with water flowing up to a pool on the surface, forms when there is no narrow channel constricting the water underground.

FUN FACTS

- In 2011, NASA's **Cassini spacecraft** flew over a geyser on Saturn's moon Enceladus while it was erupting. It was sprayed with water particles 62 miles (100 km) above the **moon's surface.**

- Saturn's moon Enceladus and Jupiter's moon Io both have the **tallest known geysers in our whole solar system.** The icy jets of water go far because the force of gravity on the moons is much weaker than Earth's gravity.

- The **largest geyser ever recorded** (on Earth) was Waimangu Geyser in New Zealand. It erupted to a height of **1,500 feet** (450 m), but it became dormant in 1904 after only four years of activity.

CRAZY COLORS

How does nature create WATERMELON SNOW, RAINBOW RIVERS, and other oddities?

Dig In

Snow is supposed to be white, rivers and lakes blue or green, and mountains ... well, mountain-colored, right? So why are there bright pink and polka-dotted lakes, watermelon-colored snow, and rivers and mountains that look like rainbows? Is nature messing with us, or what? Get ready to tour the wacky wilderness.

What made those colors **?**

Do the colors stay that way **?**

Is it safe to eat water- melon snow **?**

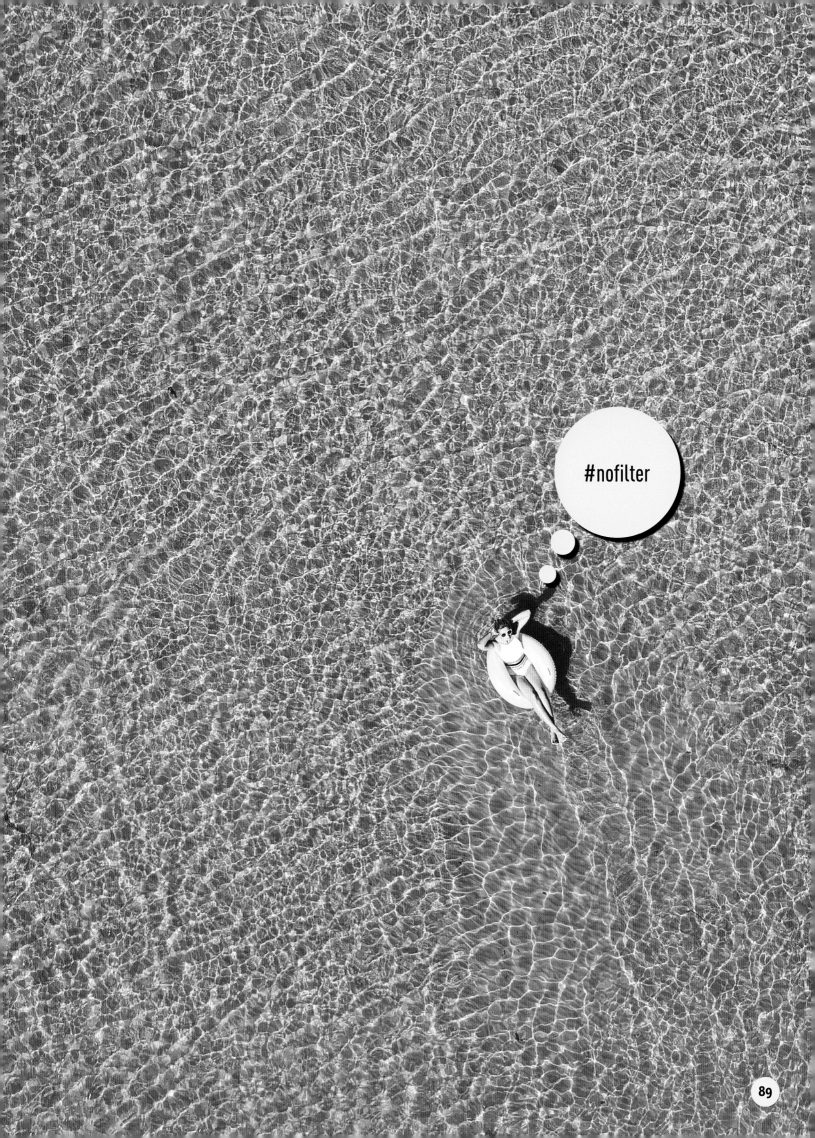

JUST THE FACTS

Supernatural

Some of the most spectacular shows in nature don't look natural at all. They're crazy colors—worthy of the wackiest Dr. Seuss book. But it wasn't an artist who created them. Sometimes it was a combination of minerals, other times it was bacteria or algae. On occasion, it was rare geological or weather conditions, or maybe just amazing plants. Take a tour and see nature's really wild side.

PRETTY POLKA DOTS

When its water evaporates in the summer, Spotted Lake (Kliluk lake) in British Columbia, Canada, becomes dotted with hundreds of yellow, green, white, and pale blue pools. From a bird's-eye view, it looks like a mosaic of shiny, multicolored stones set in concrete, but the colors actually come from unusually high concentrations of salts and other minerals.

WATERMELON POPSICLE

In high mountain ranges, such as California, U.S.A.'s Sierra Nevada, some snowbanks take on a pink tint, especially during the summer. Though snow provides hardly any nutrition for growing things, more than 60 species of algae can live in it—including a species that tints it pink. But don't eat watermelon snow! It's been known to upset tummies.

FUN FACT

FOR THOUSANDS OF YEARS, THE **OKANAGAN FIRST NATIONS** PEOPLE HAVE USED THE MINERALS IN KLILUK, OR SPOTTED LAKE, IN **HEALING CEREMONIES.**

The plains around **CAÑO CRISTALES** in Colombia are some of the richest tropical grasslands in the world. The plains are home to numerous birds of prey, capybara, anacondas, and many **CRITICALLY ENDANGERED** reptiles.

FLOWING FLORALS
Just east of the Andes Mountains in Colombia, the Caño Cristales river bursts with vibrant reds, blues, yellows, oranges, and greens. The unique river display is thanks to a very picky plant that grows only in the unusual conditions found in the river.

RAINBOW MOUNTAINS
The Rainbow Mountains in northwest China's Zhangye Danxia National Geologic Park wear multicolored stripes of reds, greens, yellows, and blues. The mountains, which are made of sandstone and siltstone, were thrust up 55 million years ago when tectonic plates crashed into each other. Weathering and erosion exposed the minerals that create the colors. A few other peaks around the world sport similar colors, but Zhangye Danxia's unique combination of varied landforms and local conditions make its mountains especially spectacular.

BUBBLE-GUM LAKE
Separated from the Atlantic Ocean only by narrow sand dunes, Lake Retba (or Lac Rose) in Senegal is distinctly pink. An extremely high salt content, salt-loving microbes, and algae give the lake its color, which ranges from a pale rose during rainy season (July through October) to bright bubble gum during the dry season (November to June).

FUN FACT

THE SPOTTED LAKE HAS A **MIX OF MINERALS** SIMILAR TO THAT OF THE COLUMBUS CRATER ON **MARS.**

WANT TO KNOW MORE?

COLOR CREATORS

Algae, microbes, pretty plants, and minerals may not seem to have a lot in common, but they go about creating wild colors in a similar way. In each of these amazing natural features, chemical reactions make use of very specific—and unusual—conditions to produce the wild colors. In both the Spotted Lake and the Rainbow Mountains, various minerals react with water and sunlight to create the colors and sculpt the features' unique shapes. In watermelon snow and Lake Retba, algae produce a pink hue as they photosynthesize, converting sunlight, water, and carbon dioxide into the energy they need to grow. The picky plant in the Caño Cristales depends on that river's unique conditions for its own photosynthesis. Colors from natural chemistry!

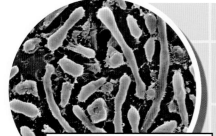

An "extremophile" microbe, a tiny creature adapted to live in extremely salty environments, helps tint some lakes pink.

FUN FACTS

● Scientists are studying the **microbes** that live in the extreme environments of **pink lakes** in hopes they might shed light on how to break down **toxic chemicals** in contaminated water.

● Local Senegalese who **harvest salt** from Lake Retba **smear their skin** with shea butter to protect it from the salty water. They get the shea butter from **shea nut trees.**

● **Pink snow** doesn't only look like watermelon, it **smells** like it! The algae that tint the snow also produce a **slightly sweet smell.**

● The word **"Danxia"** in the name of China's Zhangye Danxia National Park means **"rosy cloud."**

The REAL DEAL

Pink snow is cool—but not as cool as the regular stuff. And we're talking literally. Pink snow, that high-altitude curiosity caused by cold-loving reddish algae, melts faster than regular snow. We've known for a long time that dark colors absorb more light, while light colors reflect it. Scientists studied the pink snow and found that the red-blooming algae have the same effect: They darken the snow so it absorbs more light. Light is energy, and anything that absorbs light becomes hotter. The algae-tinted snow reflected 13 percent less light off its surface than its white counterpart. It may not be a surprising result, but it is alarming. Arctic snow-melts already are increasing with climate change. The algae may make them a bit worse—creating a vicious cycle. When snow melts, the water nourishes the algae, letting more of them grow.

Salt-loving algae produce beta-carotene— the red-orange pigment that gives carrots and flamingos their color.

LAYERED UP

The Rainbow Mountains earned their stripes over millions of years. Natural processes exposed layers and produced chemical reactions that made the colorful display.

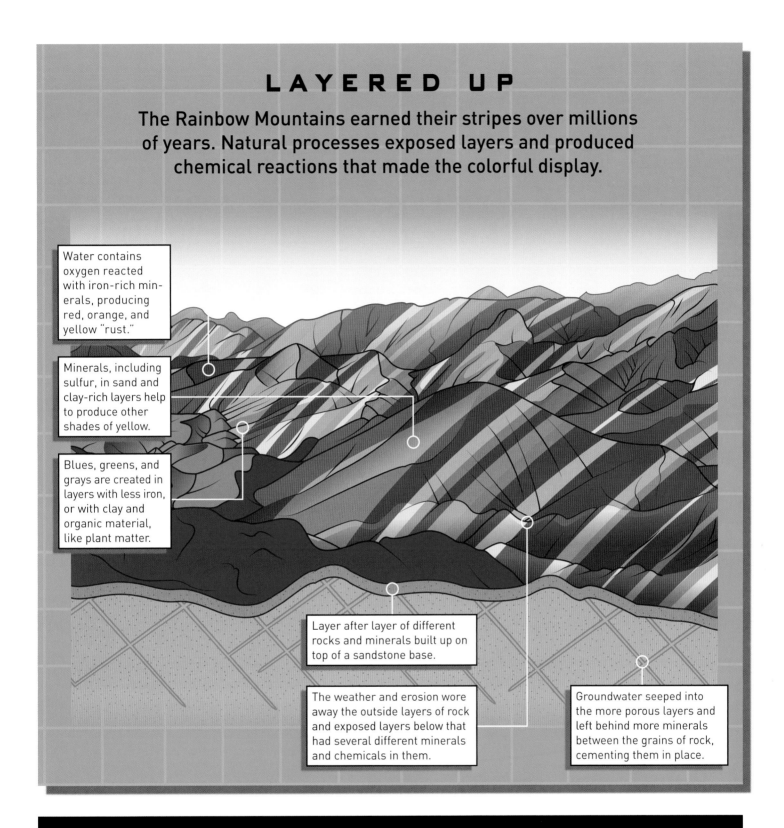

Water contains oxygen reacted with iron-rich minerals, producing red, orange, and yellow "rust."

Minerals, including sulfur, in sand and clay-rich layers help to produce other shades of yellow.

Blues, greens, and grays are created in layers with less iron, or with clay and organic material, like plant matter.

Layer after layer of different rocks and minerals built up on top of a sandstone base.

The weather and erosion wore away the outside layers of rock and exposed layers below that had several different minerals and chemicals in them.

Groundwater seeped into the more porous layers and left behind more minerals between the grains of rock, cementing them in place.

TRY THIS!

Wherever there's iron exposed to air and water, there's a good chance for rust. Iron reacts with water and oxygen in a chemical reaction called oxidation. You can see how it works with a simple experiment. Take a piece of steel wool or some nails (steel contains iron), and divide them into three glasses. Fill one glass with water, so the steel wool or nail is underwater. Pour only enough water in the second glass to come halfway up the steel wool or nail, and don't put any water in the third glass. Leave your experiment overnight and check it the next day. What happened? What does that tell you about the conditions needed to produce rust? Remember not to touch the rusty items with bare hands.

TALES FROM THE LAB

HURRICANE HUNTERS: FLYING INTO THE
EYE OF THE 1943 "SURPRISE" HURRICANE

On July 27, 1943, a powerful hurricane bore down on the upper Gulf Coast of Texas, U.S.A.—but no one was warned.

The United States and its allies were fighting in World War II, and they suspected that enemy submarines, German U-boats, lurked not far

> ## 66 THE HURRICANE POUNDED THE PLANE, TOSSING IT ABOUT. 99

offshore in the Gulf of Mexico, spying on them.

The Gulf Coast provided critical support to the Allied war effort. Oil refineries produced fuel for fighter airplanes, and shipyards built landing boats, destroyers, and minesweepers. U.S. air cadets learned to fly fighters and bombers from numerous air fields in Texas. Even British pilots trained in the region.

The Allies didn't want their enemies to learn much about their activities, so ships were operating under strict radio silence. They couldn't send messages of any kind. Unfortunately, back in those days, weather forecasters didn't have radar or satellites to help them forecast storms. They relied on ships at sea to radio in weather reports.

SOMETHING TO PROVE

During that summer, British pilots were training at Bryan Field, a hundred miles (161 km) from Houston. And they were grumbling.

They had come to learn the new technique of "flying blind," relying on the airplane's instruments to guide their flight when they couldn't see the ground. Many of the pilots already were battle-tested "Flying Aces," and they wanted to train in advanced U.S. fighter aircraft, not the slower AT-6 "Texan" trainer planes.

On the morning of July 27, word reached Bryan Field that a full-blown hurricane was heading their way. They'd need to fly their planes farther inland, out of harm's way.

The British pilots didn't know how powerful a hurricane could be. They started to tease the lead flight instructor, U.S. Air Force Col. Joe Duckworth, claiming that the "Texan" was too fragile to weather a storm—even on the tarmac.

The colonel decided to teach his British friends a lesson. He bet them he could fly the "Texan" safely right into the storm and back out, demonstrating both the plane's capabilities and the value of flying by relying on instruments. He asked Lt. Ralph O'Hair, the only navigator at the field that morning, to fly with him.

They knew headquarters would never approve the flight, so they didn't bother to ask.

They flew off into the heavy rain and darkness. The hurricane pounded the plane, tossing it about. Suddenly, they broke into the calm eye of the hurricane. There they saw bright clouds floating in a clear sky.

After circling inside, they fought their way back to the air base and landed safely. It was the first time anyone had intentionally flown into a hurricane. The air base's weather officer asked the colonel if he could go, too. The navigator was all too happy to give up his seat for the second venture into the storm.

It was another successful flight. And the British pilots never again grumbled about flying the "Texan" or using only instruments.

INSPIRATION

A year after these flights, a special air squadron, nicknamed the Hurricane Hunters, was formed to collect weather information for the government. True to their name, they'd search for hurricanes and fly into their eyes to collect weather data.

Even today, when weather forecasters can use satellites, radar, and land- and ship-based observations, they rely on the Hurricane Hunters to fly into storms to record wind direction and speed, pressure, temperature, and humidity.

It's busy work to be a Hurricane Hunter. They fly daily missions—sometimes investigating a number of storms in a single day.

HURRICANE HUNTERS USUALLY **PREFER AIRPLANES** INSTEAD OF FASTER JETS BECAUSE THE SLOWER AIRPLANES CAN **BETTER HANDLE** GETTING TOSSED AROUND BY STRONG WINDS.

Hurricane Hunters

THE **AT-6 "TEXAN"** TRAINER WASN'T AS FAST AS SOME OF THE ADVANCED FIGHTER PLANES, BUT IT WAS **NIMBLE,** ABLE TO LOOP AND TURN ON A DIME. IT'S STILL A **POPULAR PLANE** FOR AIR SHOWS.

Make It BETTER!

The Hurricane Hunters are specially trained to fly into storms. The information they collect helps weather forecasters make more accurate predictions about the strength of a storm. Still, it's dangerous to fly into a storm—even when you have special aircraft and highly skilled pilots and navigators.

How would you track the strength and path of a strong storm, like a hurricane? Can you think of a better way to collect information about strong storms? What other extreme types of weather do you think we need to study more closely, and how should we do it?

AFTER THE **"SURPRISE"** HURRICANE, WHICH KILLED **19 PEOPLE** AND INJURED HUNDREDS OF OTHERS, **STORM WARNINGS** WERE NO LONGER SILENCED— WARTIME OR NOT.

Satellites capture the swirl of a hurricane.

ROCK STAR

How was the GIANT'S CAUSEWAY created?

Dig In

On the rugged coast of Northern Ireland, 40,000 stone pillars form stepping stones so perfectly shaped that they could've been chiseled by master stonecutters. The stepping stones lead out from the cliffs and into the sea, as if retracing an ancient path to Scotland—a path laid down by a giant. Read on to learn about this wonder. It's no tall tale.

Who made the stepping stones **?**

Why are they different heights **?**

What's the deal with the giant **?**

JUST THE FACTS

Stepping Out

The 40,000 stone pillars of the Giant's Causeway are packed together, rising in multitiered stepping stones, some only a few inches (or centimeters) tall and others towering 82 feet (25 m). The columns are eerily geometric. Most are hexagonal (six-sided polygons), but others range from four to eight sides. Standing side by side in a honeycomb pattern, the columns create natural stairs and pathways along the rugged coast.

Hot Topic

The mind-blowing geology is natural. Around 60 million years ago, the region was a volcanic hotbed. Tectonic plates—the slabs of rock that make up the Earth's outer shell—drifted apart, and hot magma spewed up from inside the Earth and poured out in one lava flow after another, puddling 325 feet (100 m) thick in spots. As the lava cooled and dried into solid basalt rock, it cracked into the pillar shapes. The cracks formed first at the surface and traveled deeper into the lava as it cooled, forming the vertical columns.

PERFECT PATH

The Giant's Causeway looks like a honeycomb of multitiered stepping stones extending from the cliffs into the sea. It formed when lava cooled and cracked into geometric columns.

ROCKING OUT

The Giant's Causeway **amazes visitors** from all over the world, but it's not the only awesome **rock formation.** Take a look at these gems.

Stone Forest, China: Narrow blades of limestone—many over 33 feet (10 m) tall—jut up from what was once a shallow sea. Wind and water shaped the stone pillars.

Bryce Canyon, Utah, U.S.A.: Red spires and hoodoos—columns of weathered rock—formed when water repeatedly froze and melted in the cracks of sedimentary rock.

FUN FACT
WEATHER HAS CAUSED **CIRCLES TO APPEAR** ON THE GIANT'S CAUSEWAY FORMATIONS. MOST PEOPLE CALL THEM THE **GIANT'S EYES.**

GETTING DEEP

As the lava cooled and dried into basalt rock, cracks formed at the surface. They traveled down deeper into the lava as more of it cooled, forming tall pillars.

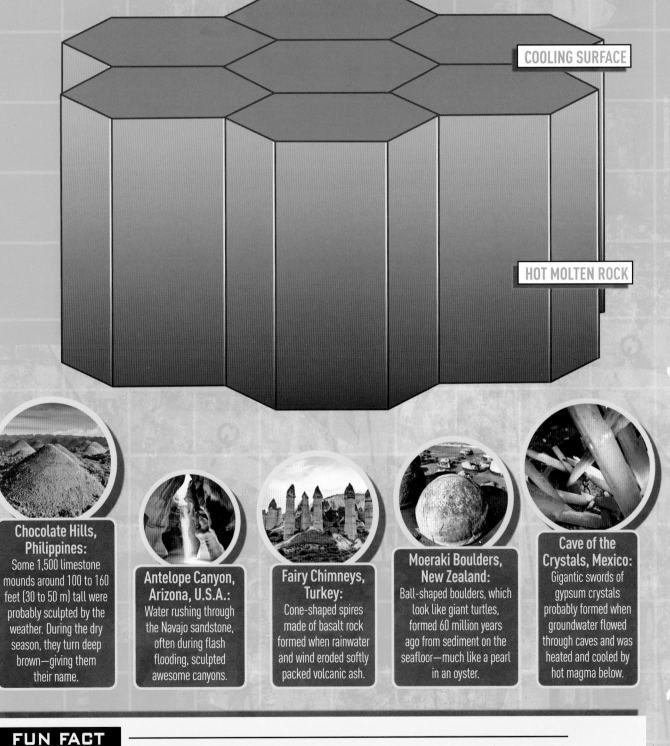

COOLING SURFACE

HOT MOLTEN ROCK

Chocolate Hills, Philippines: Some 1,500 limestone mounds around 100 to 160 feet (30 to 50 m) tall were probably sculpted by the weather. During the dry season, they turn deep brown—giving them their name.

Antelope Canyon, Arizona, U.S.A.: Water rushing through the Navajo sandstone, often during flash flooding, sculpted awesome canyons.

Fairy Chimneys, Turkey: Cone-shaped spires made of basalt rock formed when rainwater and wind eroded softly packed volcanic ash.

Moeraki Boulders, New Zealand: Ball-shaped boulders, which look like giant turtles, formed 60 million years ago from sediment on the seafloor—much like a pearl in an oyster.

Cave of the Crystals, Mexico: Gigantic swords of gypsum crystals probably formed when groundwater flowed through caves and was heated and cooled by hot magma below.

FUN FACT

THE GIANT'S CAUSEWAY BECAME INTERNATIONALLY **FAMOUS** AFTER DUBLIN ARTIST SUSANNA DRURY MADE **WATERCOLOR PAINTINGS** OF IT IN 1739. THE ART WON HER A PRIZE AND WAS REPRODUCED AS ENGRAVINGS.

WANT TO KNOW MORE?

CRACKING UP

If you've ever seen mud in a dry riverbed, you've probably noticed cracks running across and down through the surface. The columns at the Giant's Causeway formed in a similar way. As seawater washed over it, the lava cooled, dried, and contracted—decreased in size. (Hot things take up more space than cool things.) The contraction pulled one part of the newly forming rock apart from another, forming cracks. The cracks connected to each other the easiest way possible, creating the geometric pattern. Nature's artistry.

Myth vs. FACT

MYTH: An Irish giant paved the causeway to get to Scotland.

FACT: It depends on whom you ask! If you want the scientific explanation, read the rest of these pages. But if you believe in Irish mythology, you probably know of the legendary Fionn mac Cumhaill, or "Finn MacCool." Fionn was a giant among the Irish—quite literally. One day, while building a pathway across the sea to Scotland, he learned that the Scottish giant Benandonner wanted to challenge him. Fionn was a gentle giant and, as it turns out, not nearly as big as his Scottish rival. Luckily, Fionn hatched a plan with his cunning wife, Oonagh. Oonagh dressed Fionn in a nightshirt and bonnet and laid him in a massive cradle. When Benandonner arrived at their home, she said her husband was out but that she and their "baby" expected him back shortly. Benandonner was welcome to wait. The Scottish giant peeked into the cradle and panicked. If Fionn's baby was so large, how big would Fionn himself be?! Benandonner ran back to Scotland, destroying the causeway behind him to make sure that Fionn would not follow.

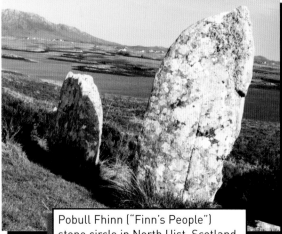

Pobull Fhinn ("Finn's People") stone circle in North Uist, Scotland

DEEP DIVISIONS

As the newly forming basalt rock cooled, each column contracted, or shrank, into cool geometric shapes.

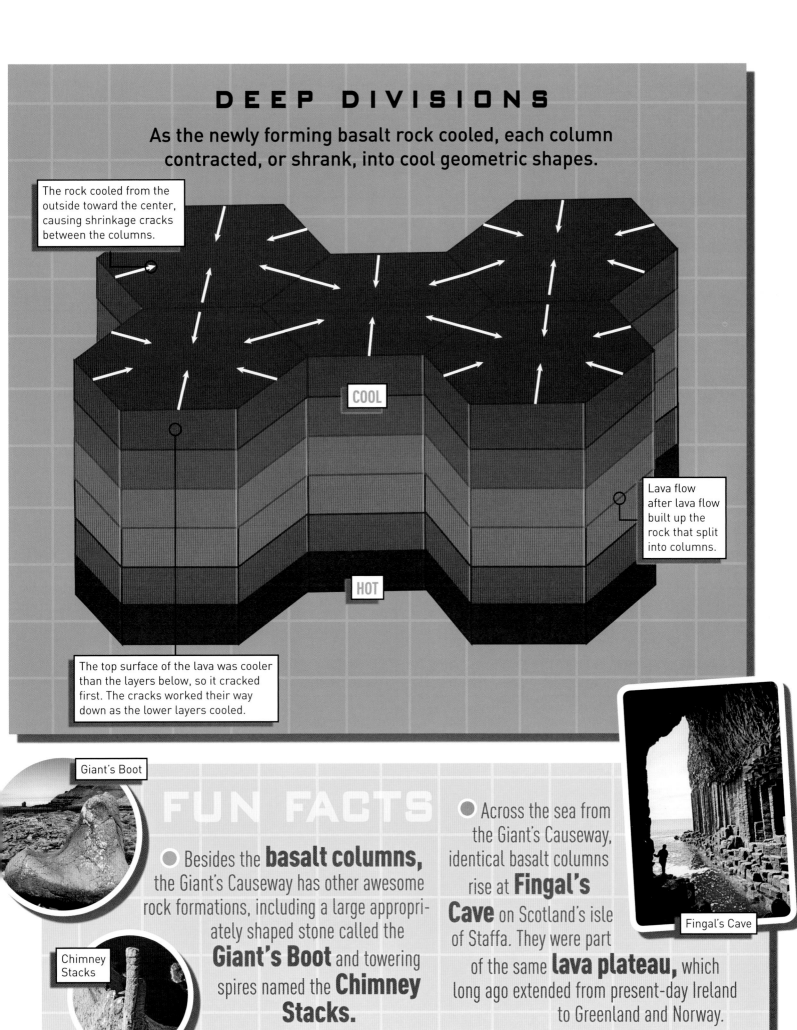

The rock cooled from the outside toward the center, causing shrinkage cracks between the columns.

COOL

HOT

Lava flow after lava flow built up the rock that split into columns.

The top surface of the lava was cooler than the layers below, so it cracked first. The cracks worked their way down as the lower layers cooled.

Giant's Boot

FUN FACTS

● Besides the **basalt columns,** the Giant's Causeway has other awesome rock formations, including a large appropriately shaped stone called the **Giant's Boot** and towering spires named the **Chimney Stacks.**

Chimney Stacks

● Across the sea from the Giant's Causeway, identical basalt columns rise at **Fingal's Cave** on Scotland's isle of Staffa. They were part of the same **lava plateau,** which long ago extended from present-day Ireland to Greenland and Norway.

Fingal's Cave

DOING THE TWIST

How does a **TORNADO** become so powerful?

Dig In

Just ask Dorothy and Toto: Tornadoes have the power to wreak havoc as they roar across the land, smashing buildings and uprooting trees. The fearsome funnel clouds are a scary sight but also an awesome example of how weather conditions combine to create bizarre phenomena. Come on, let's take a look inside a twister—from a safe distance.

How does it form **?**

How do you predict a tornado **?**

How strong is it **?**

Swirling Fury

Tornadoes are violent, swirling funnel-shaped clouds that stretch from a thunderstorm to the ground. They can be skinny or a mile (1.5 km) wide at their base and as tall as 11 miles (18 km) high. While some tornadoes touch down only for a few seconds or minutes, others cut a path of destruction for hours. Even the "weak" tornadoes—fortunately, about two-thirds of all tornadoes—can have winds as strong as 110 miles an hour (177 km/h). "Strong" tornadoes—about a third of tornadoes—have winds reaching 205 miles an hour (330 km/h). The worst are "violent tornadoes."

Touch Down

Tornadoes form inside some thunderstorms. Warm, moist air near the ground's surface crashes into cool, dry air higher up, creating unstable conditions. Winds blow from different directions in the unstable conditions, creating a spinning effect that rises up inside the storm. The swirling thunderstorm may drop a funnel-shaped cloud to the ground—the tornado.

TORNADO
WANNABES

Nothing matches the power of a tornado, but it's not the only swirling bit of weather. Take a look at these little twisters.

Dust devil: Despite its scary name, it's a small, usually harmless swirling plume of dust. It forms on hot, dry days when hot air rises and rotates.

Gustnado: Usually lasting only a few minutes, it's a dust cloud that swirls below a thunderstorm but does not reach up into the cloud. Since it comes with a storm, people often mistake it for a tornado.

Waterspout: Most common along the Gulf Coast, it's a weak tornado that forms over the sea, picking up water and spinning it into a moving column.

Landspout: As its name suggests, it's a waterspout over land. It's like a very weak tornado, but it does not form from a mesocyclone as tornadoes do.

Sharknado: Just kidding. There's no such thing in real life! It was a funny sci-fi flick about a waterspout that lifted sharks out of the ocean and dropped them into the streets of Los Angeles.

FUN FACT

HOW FAR DO TORNADOES CARRY OBJECTS THEY SUCK UP? THINGS ARE USUALLY DROPPED WITHIN 15 TO 20 MILES (24 TO 32 KM) OF WHERE THEY STARTED. BUT RESEARCHERS HAVE FOUND ITEMS CARRIED MORE THAN 150 MILES (240 KM) AWAY.

TORNADO GENERATOR

Most tornadoes form from severe thunderstorms with extremely unstable wind conditions.

COLD AND HOT AIR
Thunderstorms form when hot, humid air near the ground rises into cold, dry air higher up.

SIDE WINDS
Winds blowing from different directions at different heights cause air rising into the thunderstorm to spin, creating the kind of storm capable of producing tornadoes.

HOT AIR

FUNNEL
In some storms, a funnel cloud drops down from the storm cloud and becomes a tornado.

CLOUD OF DEBRIS
When the funnel cloud reaches the ground, it creates a whirling cloud of dust and debris.

Tornadoes are powerful enough to turn forks and knives into **DEADLY MISSILES,** but they probably can't drive a single piece of straw into a tree trunk—no matter what you've heard.

FUN FACT
"TORNADO ALLEY," A REGION EXTENDING ACROSS THE CENTRAL PLAINS IN NORTH AMERICA, PRODUCES MORE TORNADOES THAN ANY OTHER **PLACE ON EARTH.**

WANT TO KNOW MORE?

Not every storm produces a tornado, of course. (Whew!) Tornadoes are most likely to form in powerful storms called supercells. Scientists still don't know exactly why some supercells produce tornadoes and others don't, but they've identified several necessary ingredients. Warm air rises, creating a strong upward draft. As the air climbs, it can change direction and whip around quickly. A vortex, a tube of spinning air, can form and get pulled upward, creating a "mesocyclone" inside the storm. Cooler, dryer air sinks down behind the mesocyclone, creating a downdraft. The updrafts and downdrafts keep the conditions unstable. If the funnel cloud moves down into the large, moist bottom of the storm, it can become a tornado. Besides producing violent tornadoes, supercells can produce heavy rain, lightning, and hail.

How Things Worked

In 1888, the first attempt to forecast tornadoes was cut short. The word "tornado" was banned from official weather forecasts by the U.S. Army Signal Corps, which had led the study of how tornadoes formed. The corps' weather-watching network was limited, and officials didn't want people to panic at the mention of tornadoes. The ban on using the word "tornado" lasted into the 1900s, even after the deadly Tri-State Tornado of 1925. But after 132 tornadoes ripped through America in 1942, the Weather Bureau knew things had to change. It experimented with warning systems in Kansas and Missouri. Local weather observers started forecasting when conditions might create storms, but they couldn't give exact times or locations. In the late 1940s, U.S. Navy officers made a big breakthrough, developing a technique to predict tornadoes. They made the first tornado forecast in 1948, saving lives at a U.S. Air Force base in Oklahoma. But their forecasts only went out to the Air Force. By 1950, the Weather Bureau used radar, developed a few years earlier during World War II, to forecast severe weather and in the mid-1960s added satellite imagery, too. Over the next decades, it added better technology and developed effective warning systems. Tornadoes travel an unpredictable path, but forecasters can now give enough advanced warning for people to get to safety.

TRY THIS!

You don't need to be a storm chaser to see a tornado. It's a lot easier—and safer—to create your own. Grab two clean and empty two-liter bottles and fill about two-thirds of one bottle with water. Flip the second bottle over and duct tape it to the top of the partially filled bottle, so their openings are together. Use enough tape so no water leaks out! Now turn your "tornado maker" over so the water is on the top and give it a good circular swirl to get things going. The swirling motion creates a vortex like a tornado.

A supercell is a powerful rotating storm that can produce a tornado.

DESTRUCTIVE FORCE

A supercell may look a bit like other thunderstorms, but it doesn't act like them. It rotates, creating the possibility of strong, destructive tornadoes. About one-third of supercells produce tornadoes.

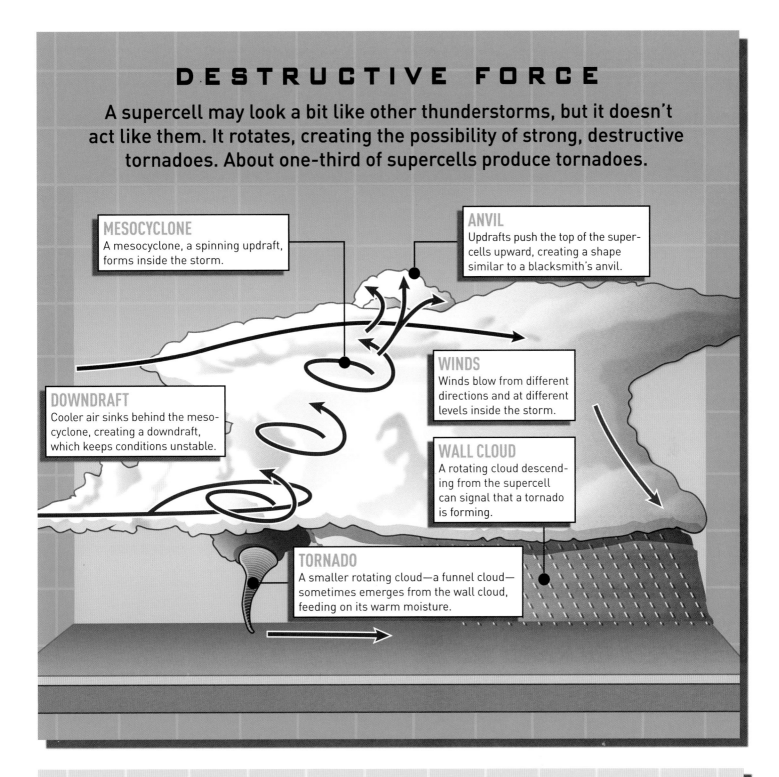

MESOCYCLONE
A mesocyclone, a spinning updraft, forms inside the storm.

ANVIL
Updrafts push the top of the super-cells upward, creating a shape similar to a blacksmith's anvil.

DOWNDRAFT
Cooler air sinks behind the meso-cyclone, creating a downdraft, which keeps conditions unstable.

WINDS
Winds blow from different directions and at different levels inside the storm.

WALL CLOUD
A rotating cloud descend-ing from the supercell can signal that a tornado is forming.

TORNADO
A smaller rotating cloud—a funnel cloud—sometimes emerges from the wall cloud, feeding on its warm moisture.

FUN FACTS
AND NOT-SO-FUN FACTS

● They sky sometimes turns a **sickly grayish green** color when a tornado is on the way. It's because severe thunderstorms carry a **lot of water,** which scatters red light waves but lets the greenish ones pass through.

● People who've **survived** torna-does often say they sound like the **roar of a freight train** passing by.

● The **most destruc-tive** tornado in the United States was the **Tri-State Tornado** of March 18, 1925. The half-mile (1-km)-wide funnel tore 219 miles (352 km) across Missouri, Illinois, and Indiana, **leveling towns** and killing 695 people.

PROFILE: David Gruber

MARINE BIOLOGIST

If an eel hadn't photo-bombed David Gruber's shot of coral, David may have missed the discovery of a lifetime.

David, an expert on coral, was diving with his team near the Cayman Islands. They wanted to photograph fluorescent coral deep in the ocean. This coral seems to glow by transforming blue ocean light into other colors, like green, orange, or red. To get the shots, David had to duct tape a special blue filter over his camera's flash and

> **"SOMEBODY'S GOT TO GO DOWN AND CHECK TO SEE IF THE SHARKS ARE FLUORESCENT."**

another over his lens, so his camera would "see" the colors being transformed by the corals.

When they got back and looked at their photos, they saw what looked like an eel in one of the pictures. But it wasn't your typical eel. This one was tiny, about the length of a finger, and it was green. Glowing green.

"We're rubbing our eyes, checking the filters, thinking that somebody's maybe playing a joke on us with the camera," David recalls. "But the eel was real."

It was an amazing discovery: the first green fluorescent fish

ever seen. David wondered if there were others. He teamed up with a fish scientist and began searching reefs around the world. What they found surpassed their wildest imaginations.

ALIEN WORLD

It turns out that there's a whole world of glowing sea creatures in the ocean.

To find them, David and his partners had to see life in the ocean the way fish do. The ocean acts like a humongous filter, screening out light rays of most colors but leaving blue. Biofluorescent creatures take in that blue light, transform it, and give off other, glowing colors.

If divers use white lights, they'll miss the amazing light show that fish see. So David's team designed new camera gear and lights that gave off the right kind of blue light. Then they went diving.

They found their photo-bombing eel. Then they found many others—more than 200 species of biofluorescent fish, plus red-glowing seahorses, biofluorescent sea turtles, and stingrays that glowed green.

That got them thinking. If there are glowing stingrays, what about sharks?

"Somebody's got to go down and check to see if the sharks are fluorescent," David says.

In a deep, dark canyon off the California coast, they found the first biofluorescent shark. The swellshark twinkled with spots and stunning patterns that glowed in blue light.

It was mind-blowing. But David knew there must be a reason for the shark's good looks. The team contacted an eye specialist to study the shark's vision. They discovered that the swellshark can only see blue-green, but it sees those colors amazingly well. David then made a "shark-eye camera." It showed that the sharks see other glowing sharks much better than they can see non-fluorescent sharks. It's like having a secret channel that allows them to better spot each other.

DEEPENING THE SEARCH

David pushed deeper into the ocean. He saw biolumines-cent creatures, which create their own flashing and lights.

Seeing their light shows requires special equipment. So David and his team made a robotic undersea vehicle. He can drive it around the deep, dark sea using almost no lights to capture the creatures' bioluminescence without disturbing them.

David never tires of the adventure. He wants others to share his passion, too. "There is a whole world on a living reef, and it's elaborate and bustling like a busy city beneath the waves, just waiting to be explored."

DAVID GOT INTERESTED IN MARINE BIOLOGY **SURFING** IN HAWAII IN HIS TEENS. WHILE HE WAS SURFING, HE BEGAN TO WONDER ABOUT THE **LIFE UNDERNEATH THE WAVES.**

a biofluorescent eel

GLOWING SEA CREATURES ARE NOT ONLY AMAZING TO LOOK AT. THE PROTEIN THAT MAKES THEM GLOW CAN HELP SCIENTISTS AND DOCTORS **FIGHT DISEASES** IN PEOPLE. IT HELPS LIGHT UP HARD-TO-SEE PROBLEMS, LIKE CANCER CELLS OR NERVE DAMAGE IN BRAINS.

yellow stingray

SWELLSHARKS GET THEIR NAME FROM THEIR ABILITY TO GULP DOWN WATER AND **PUFF THEMSELVES UP** TWICE THEIR USUAL SIZE. IT HELPS KEEP THEM SAFE.

swellshark

LIGHT SHOW

How do the NORTHERN LIGHTS color the night sky?

Dig In

Waves of neon green, purple, red, or blue light dance across the northern night sky on some nights. They're the aurora borealis, or northern lights, one of Earth's most awesome displays. Along with its southern cousin, the aurora australis, the northern lights have mystified and delighted humans for centuries. Wonder how the auroras work? Stick around, and we'll enlighten you.

Where do the lights come from ?

How do they get their colors ?

Why can't you see them everywhere ?

JUST THE FACTS

Bright Nights

It takes both the sun and Earth's atmosphere to produce the brilliant light shows known as the aurora borealis and aurora australis. Electrically charged particles from solar winds collide with the various gases in Earth's atmosphere, causing the gases to light up and glow for anywhere from a few minutes to several hours. The color of the lights depends on the type of gas. Oxygen produces red and green colors higher in the sky, while nitrogen produces the pink, purple, and blue lights at lower levels.

Magnetic Attraction

The auroras form in the north and south—roughly around the Arctic and Antarctic Circles—because of the magnetic field surrounding Earth. The electrically charged particles get trapped in the magnetic field and follow it down to the Earth's magnetic north and south poles. It's easiest to see the light shows if you're in the far north (or far south, but there's less land there), but on occasion, they can be seen farther away. The display is so brilliant that people sometimes travel just to see them. The best times to see them are during chilly months in the far north when the nights are long and dark.

MYSTERY SOLVED?

If we humans see something mystifying, we want to know what caused it. It's **part of our nature.** So way back before scientists figured out how the northern lights formed, various peoples came up with more mystical explanations for the **mysterious phenomenon.**

The **Vikings** believed that Valkyries—mythical, immortal female figures who chose who died in battle and who lived—galloped across the sky on their horses, leaving the light from their shimmering armor trailing behind them.

Inuit believed the lights to be the souls of seals, salmon, whales, and deer that they had hunted.

The **Menominee** people, Native Americans living in the Great Lakes region of North America, suspected the lights came from torches of giants who lived farther north.

Europeans in the Middle Ages thought the shimmering lights were messages from God.

FUN FACT —

AS EARLY AS 2600 B.C., CHINESE ACCOUNTS SPOKE OF THE **NORTHERN LIGHTS,** CALLING THEM **"STRONG LIGHTNING"** THAT ILLUMINATED THE WHOLE SKY.

WORTH A TRIP

The aurora borealis fills the northern skies with brilliant colors, thanks to solar winds bringing electrically charged particles into the Earth's atmosphere. The electrical charges react with Earth's magnetic forces in shifting patterns, causing the aurora's colors to dance across the sky.

The aurora borealis changes shape in the sky.

FUN FACT

EARTH ISN'T THE ONLY PLANET WITH THIS **COSMIC LIGHT SHOW.** AURORAS HAVE BRIGHTENED THE SKIES AROUND **JUPITER, SATURN, URANUS, VENUS,** AND **NEPTUNE**—AS WELL AS SOME OF THEIR MOONS.

WANT TO KNOW MORE?

TELL ME MORE

SOLAR POWERED

The sun is a power plant. It generates temperatures so high that they can break down atoms—the little bits that make up everything—into their component parts: protons and electrically charged electrons. Solar winds carry some of these particles to Earth. The magnetic shield around Earth's atmosphere deflects most of the charged particles, but some get trapped in the magnetic field and follow it to the North and South Poles. There, the electrons crash into gas molecules in Earth's atmosphere, causing them to emit bursts of light—the auroras.

Whoa... SLOW DOWN! A Closer Look at Light

How does a collision between electrons and gas molecules create light? The electrons get excited. Really, that's a term scientists use when electrons jump up a level in energy. Normally, electrons are zipping around the outside of an atom's nucleus. They want to stay in their orbits. But if energetic particles crash into each other, the electrons absorb some of that energy and jump up a level to a higher orbit—but only for a moment. When the electrons relax and return to their normal orbit, or level of activity, they let go of the extra energy. It comes out as a burst of light, a photon. It's like their little sigh of relaxation.

SPACE TRAVELERS

It takes a huge release of energy from the sun to start the creation of the auroras here on Earth.

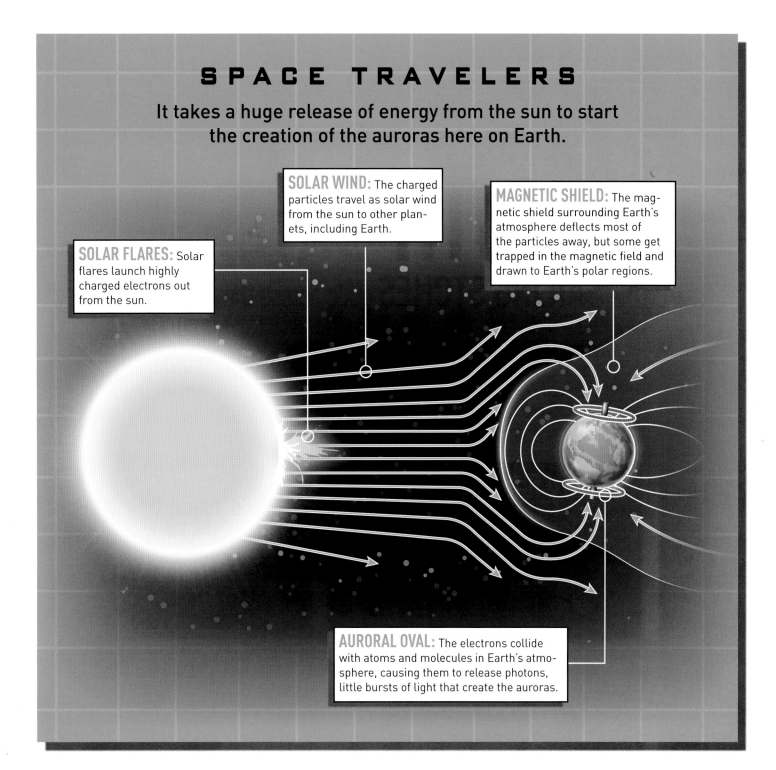

SOLAR WIND: The charged particles travel as solar wind from the sun to other planets, including Earth.

MAGNETIC SHIELD: The magnetic shield surrounding Earth's atmosphere deflects most of the particles away, but some get trapped in the magnetic field and drawn to Earth's polar regions.

SOLAR FLARES: Solar flares launch highly charged electrons out from the sun.

AURORAL OVAL: The electrons collide with atoms and molecules in Earth's atmosphere, causing them to release photons, little bursts of light that create the auroras.

FUN FACTS

● The northern lights **vary in strength.** Sometimes they're a faint glow, but other times they shine so brightly that **you could read a book** in the middle of the night. We'd suggest you look up instead.

● On September 1, 1859, telegraph communications on Earth were **knocked out,** and the nighttime skies lit up with auroras more brilliant than ever seen before. Some people thought the **world was ending,** but astronomer Richard Carrington knew what really happened. Earlier that day, he had discovered **solar flares.** The resulting solar storm was the largest on record.

SMOOTH SAILING

How do the SAILING STONES glide across the desert?

Dig In

On the dry flat lands of Death Valley, in California's Mojave Desert, stones weighing as much as a piano slide across the cracked mud, leaving their long tracks behind them. The ground next to them is not disturbed—no tire tracks, no footprints, no signs that aliens landed a spaceship nearby. So how do they move?

Are the stones really sailing?

How did scientists solve the mystery?

Why does it happen in Death Valley?

Sneaky Stones

Imagine it: stones, ranging in size from a baseball to a microwave oven or larger, drift across Racetrack Playa, a flat, dried-up lake bed ringed by mountains. Judging by the tracks they leave etched in the cracked dirt, some have moved a few feet (about a meter) while others have traveled the length of an entire football field. But no one caught them in the act until 2013—a fact that, for decades, only added to their mystery.

Slip Sliding Away

The secret to the stones' moving actually is ice, wind, and water. In the winter, the temperatures at Racetrack Playa can dip really low. If water is on the ground, it freezes overnight into ice. The ice cracks into thin sheets, which act like sails in the wind, pushing against the rocks and causing them to skim along the slushy water. It only takes a slight breeze to send them sailing, with the stones dragging trails in the soft mud below. Mystery solved!

The **SAILING STONES** take advantage of ice "sails" to glide along the surface of **RACE-TRACK PLAYA** when it's wet. On the way, they drag a bit in the mud, leaving tracks of their journeys.

EPIC FAILS

Since the stones were discovered in 1948, people have come up with a **variety of explanations** for the mysterious movements. Some theories got it partly right, but none put it all together (until 2013). Other ideas were just plain weird! Here are "explanations" that failed to explain the sailing stones.

Ice rafts: Small sheets of ice boost the rocks up enough that they can skim along on a surface of water when the wind blows. (So close! All the ingredients are there, but the rocks aren't grabbing a ride on little rafts.)

Dust devils and flooding: The swirling plumes of dust move the rocks along a water-soaked surface. (No, those winds aren't strong enough.)

Strong winds and water: Really strong gusts of wind blow the stones over rain-moistened soil. (Again, no. There'd still be too much friction from the ground.)

Big ice sheet and wind: A massive ice sheet locks all the stones in a formation and glides forward, thanks to the wind. (Sorry, the stones don't actually move in parallel formation.)

Energy fields: Earth's magnetic field—or some mysterious energy—pulls the stones. (No, the magnetic field is no different there than in other places where rocks don't budge. As for mysterious energy … not proven!)

Aliens: Aliens fly down in their spaceships and move them—maybe just to mess with us. (Yeah, right. We're not even going to comment on that idea.)

Magic: The sailing stones just will themselves to move along the playa. (Or maybe a bunny leaps out of a magician's hat, hops on over, and blows on them. We think not.)

Death Valley is one of the most scorching places on Earth. Summer temperatures reach 120 degrees Fahrenheit (49 degrees Celsius)—or higher. But Racetrack Playa sits at a high elevation, more than two-thirds of a mile (1,130 m) above sea level. On rare occasions in the winter, the weather creates the right conditions for the stones to go sailing. If it rains or snows, the playa can become a shallow lake.

Low overnight temperatures can freeze the water into ice, which then cracks during a sunny day. The ice panels, as thin as a windowpane, float along in a breeze and on the flowing water, pushing the stones ahead of them.

SLICK TRICK

It takes the right weather conditions to come together for the sailing stones to make their move across Racetrack Playa.

RAIN: The playa, usually parched in the desert climate, receives enough rain to create a shallow lake.

ICE: Temperatures dip low enough to freeze the water before it has a chance to evaporate in the sun.

SUN: The ice cracks under the morning sun into thin sheets.

WIND: Wind blows the floating ice sheets across the top of the shallow water.

SAILS: The ice sheets bump into the stones and act like "sails," sliding them over the slushy surface.

Whoa ... SLOW DOWN!
A Closer Look at Ice

Why does ice float on water? Usually solid objects are denser and have more weight than liquids, so the solid objects sink. But ice, which is the solid state of water, doesn't sink; it floats. So what's up (literally) with ice? Ice's floating trick has to do with the molecules that it's made of. Have you heard water referred to as H_2O? That means it's made of hydrogen (H) and oxygen (O). When water freezes, its molecules slow down enough that their bonds hold them in fixed positions. In water's case, the hydrogen bonds adjust to hold the oxygen atoms farther apart than when they're in a liquid state. Since they're more spread out, ice ends up being less dense than water. And that's a good thing for the sailing stones on Racetrack Playa. If ice didn't float, they wouldn't move.

FUN FACTS

● To test their theory that **powerful winds** pushed the stones across a flooded surface, early researchers soaked part of the playa and used a plane's propeller to create the wind. Their test **failed to prove** their case.

● One team of researchers, who tracked the movements of 30 stones twice a year, **gave them all names.** The most impressive boulder, a 700-pound (318-kg) beauty, was named **Karen.**

● Ice can **float boulders** onto Arctic beaches—a fact that clued in scientists to how the **sailing stones** could move.

TRY THIS!

STORM SENSOR

MAKE YOUR OWN WEATHER BAROMETER

Meteorologists, the people who study and predict weather, use a lot of gadgets to make forecasts. One of the most useful is a barometer, an instrument that measures air pressure. Changes in air pressure often signal the arrival of fair or foul weather. It doesn't take a high-tech barometer to see the changes. You can make one using simple materials. Get ready to forecast.

WHAT YOU NEED

TIME: about half an hour (and longer to forecast)

1. Wide-mouthed glass jar
2. Balloon (round)
3. Rubber band
4. Scissors
5. Small stirring stick or drinking straw
6. Glue or tape
7. Piece of card stock, index card, or manila folder
8. Ruler
9. Pen or pencil
10. Box

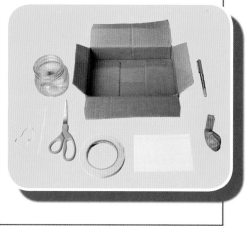

WHAT TO DO

1. CUT OFF THE NECK of the balloon, leaving only the top.

2. STRETCH THE BALLOON TOP tightly over the top of the jar and hold it in place with the rubber band. (Note: The seal must be airtight, so make sure the rubber band is tight.)

3. GLUE OR TAPE THE stirring stick (or straw) to the middle of the balloon so that most of it sticks out to the side.

4. STAND YOUR PIECE OF card stock, index card, or manila folder up inside your box. (Tip: Either fold it so it can stand on its own or tape it to the inside of the box.)

5. PLACE YOUR BAROMETER INSIDE the box so the stirring stick (or straw) points at—but does not touch—the card stock (or other paper). Mark a line on the card stock at that level. Above the line, write "high pressure"; below it, write "low pressure." This is your scale.

6. TAPE THE BAROMETER and scale in place in the box so they can't move.

7. LOOK AT THE SCALE every day and see if the stirring stick points higher or lower than the day before. (Tip: Mark where it points every day so it's easier to tell if it moves.)

MEMORY AID: When the air pressure drops, something drops out of the sky—rain or snow.

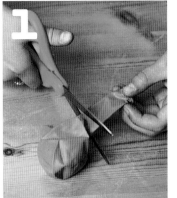

ITALIAN INVENTOR EVANGELISTA TORRICELLI, ONE OF GALILEO'S STUDENTS, INVENTED THE BAROMETER IN THE MID-1640s. THE FIRST BAROMETERS WERE MADE OF TALL, CLOSED GLASS TUBES STANDING UPSIDE DOWN IN LIQUID. CHANGES IN AIR PRESSURE MADE THE LIQUID RISE OR FALL INSIDE THE TUBE.

WHAT TO EXPECT

HIGH PRESSURE WILL MAKE THE BALLOON DIP DOWN A LITTLE, CAUSING THE STRAW TO POINT HIGHER. LOW PRESSURE WILL MAKE THE BALLOON PUFF UP A BIT, CAUSING THE STRAW TO POINT LOWER.

WHAT'S GOING ON?

AIR HAS WEIGHT, AND IT PRESSES DOWN ON EARTH. WE'RE USED TO THE FEELING, SO WE DON'T EVEN THINK ABOUT IT. BUT IT EXISTS, AND WE REFER TO IT AS AIR PRESSURE. AIR PRESSURE DOESN'T STAY THE SAME. WHEN AIR COOLS, IT FALLS, INCREASING THE AIR PRESSURE CLOSER TO THE GROUND (WHERE WE TYPICALLY MEASURE IT). HIGHER AIR PRESSURE USUALLY MEANS CLEAR WEATHER. WHEN THE AIR WARMS UP AND RISES, AIR PRESSURE NEAR THE GROUND DECREASES. WHEN THE PRESSURE DROPS, IT OFTEN MEANS CLOUDY, RAINY (OR SNOWY), OR STORMY WEATHER IS ON THE WAY.

CHAPTER 4

I SCREAM, YOU SCREAM

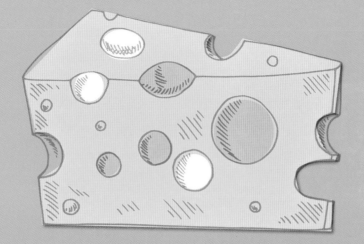

WE ALL SCREAM FOR ... WAIT, WAIT, WAIT.

Were you singing along? 'Cause we couldn't hear you. (Maybe we were just distracted.) Anyway, we hope you were belting out that song because food is something to celebrate—and not just because it's yummy. It's amazing! It's a shape-shifter. Kernels burst into fluffy popcorn, tiny sugar crystals puff up into sweet clouds, milk transforms into yogurt. And then, of course, there's ice cream. It's time to explore some culinary creations so delectable, they'll make you want to shout. Or scream. Whatever.

SPACE CASE

How is FREEZE-DRIED ICE CREAM made?

Dig In

It's often called astronaut ice cream, and it's no wonder why. Crunchy freeze-dried ice cream melts in your mouth into a sweet treat, tasting a lot like the scooped-up stuff. It's the kind of lightweight treat we imagine astronauts would love. But how does freezing-cold, soft ice cream become a brittle, chunky treat? Buckle up, we're going to explore this cosmic delight.

Why is it so lightweight ?

How is the ice cream dried ?

Why doesn't it melt ?

JUST THE FACTS

Freeze ...

In its traditional form, ice cream is a frozen treat made when you whip together cream, sweeteners, and flavorings and churn them—or turn them over and over—in the frozen container of an ice-cream maker. If you could see inside ice cream, you'd notice little ice crystals, air bubbles, and fat droplets from the cream, all held together in a sugary solution.

... Dried

Freeze-drying occurs in a special vacuum chamber, which controls the temperature and pressure. When both are low enough, the ice crystals in ice cream evaporate, turning directly into vapor (and skipping right over melting). The rest of ice cream's structure is left intact. When you take a bite of freeze-dried ice cream, the water in your mouth replaces some of the ice cream's moisture, making it more like the traditional treat.

Space Saver

When you remove its water, food ends up much lighter, so it's easier to carry. Plus, it won't spoil because bacteria, which need water to live, can't grow on it. Space-age packaging keeps moisture out.

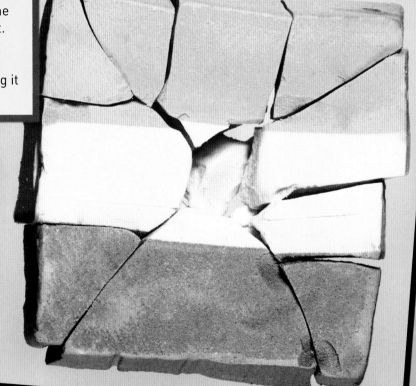

FUN FACT

ASTRONAUTS NEVER ATE "ASTRONAUT ICE CREAM." IT'S **TOO CRUMBLY** FOR MICROGRAVITY. THE CRUMBS WOULD FLOAT AROUND AND **BE A RISK** TO ASTRONAUTS, WHO MIGHT ACCIDENTALLY BREATHE THEM IN.

ASTRONAUT ICE-CREAM MAKER

Freeze-drying ice cream requires the perfect combination of low temperature and low pressure so ice can turn directly into vapor and leave the ice cream, resulting in the crispy treat.

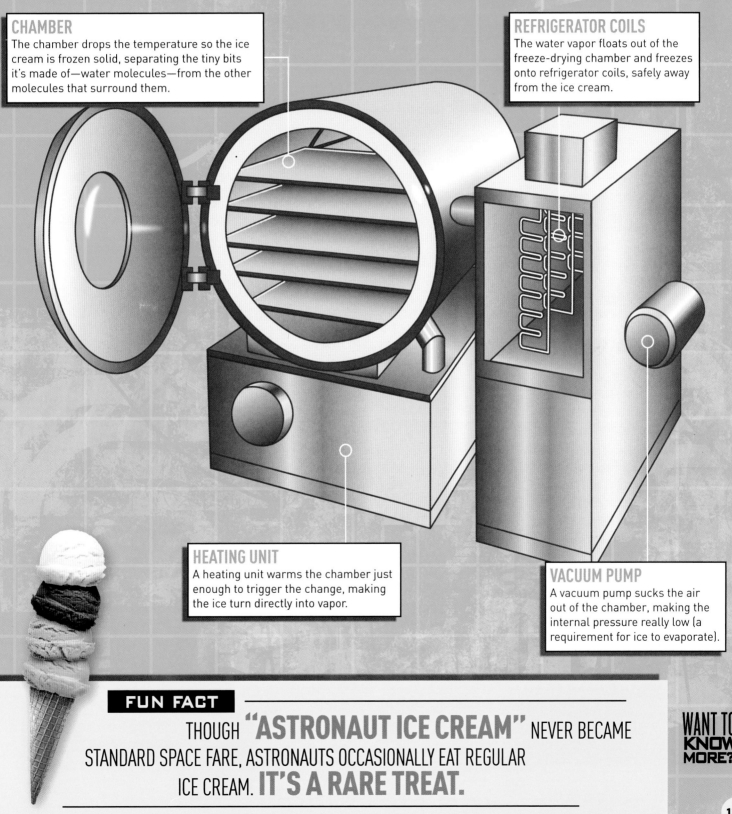

CHAMBER
The chamber drops the temperature so the ice cream is frozen solid, separating the tiny bits it's made of—water molecules—from the other molecules that surround them.

REFRIGERATOR COILS
The water vapor floats out of the freeze-drying chamber and freezes onto refrigerator coils, safely away from the ice cream.

HEATING UNIT
A heating unit warms the chamber just enough to trigger the change, making the ice turn directly into vapor.

VACUUM PUMP
A vacuum pump sucks the air out of the chamber, making the internal pressure really low (a requirement for ice to evaporate).

FUN FACT

THOUGH "ASTRONAUT ICE CREAM" NEVER BECAME STANDARD SPACE FARE, ASTRONAUTS OCCASIONALLY EAT REGULAR ICE CREAM. IT'S A RARE TREAT.

WANT TO KNOW MORE?

SIMPLY SUBLIME

Going straight from ice to vapor is an amazing feat, called sublimation. (Remember that, usually, frozen ice melts into liquid water, which must boil to become vapor, water's gaseous phase.) Each state of water (ice, liquid, or vapor) requires specific combinations of temperature and pressure. Liquid water must have temperatures above freezing plus a good amount of pressure. If you use a vacuum chamber to keep the pressure really low, liquid water won't be able to form no matter what. If you raise the temperature above the freezing point while keeping the pressure really low, the ice will thaw—but go straight to vapor.

WHOA ... SLOW DOWN!
A Closer Look at Freeze-Drying

People have been preserving food by removing its water, or dehydrating it, since prehistoric times. Back then, food was usually set in the sun for long periods until its water evaporated and the food dried out. Many foods still can be dehydrated this way or by using other forms of heat (often in some gadget). So what's the difference between "regular" dehydration and freeze-drying? Heat.

Heat energy triggers chemical reactions in food, affecting its appearance, smell, and taste. A lot of times, that's great. That's why we cook! But if you use heat mainly to dehydrate a food, it won't spring back exactly to its original form when you add water. That's not so much the case with freeze-drying. Freeze-drying doesn't rely on heat to cause evaporation, and so it doesn't trigger the chemical reactions that change the food. Besides, heat-based dehydration doesn't work for all foods. Imagine what it'd do to ice cream!

TRY THIS!

If you can get your hands on astronaut ice cream (also called space ice cream), definitely try it out! But even if you can't find that freeze-dried treat, you can have some delicious fun with freeze-dried fruit or veggies. You can get those from most grocery stores. Taste them in their freeze-dried state. Then do a little experiment. Weigh a piece. Then soak it in water for a couple of hours, take it out of the water and weigh it again. What happened when you added the water back to the food (rehydrated it)? How did it taste?

SHAPE-SHIFTER

When we think of ice changing into a different state, we usually imagine it melting into liquid water. But under the right conditions, it can change directly into vapor.

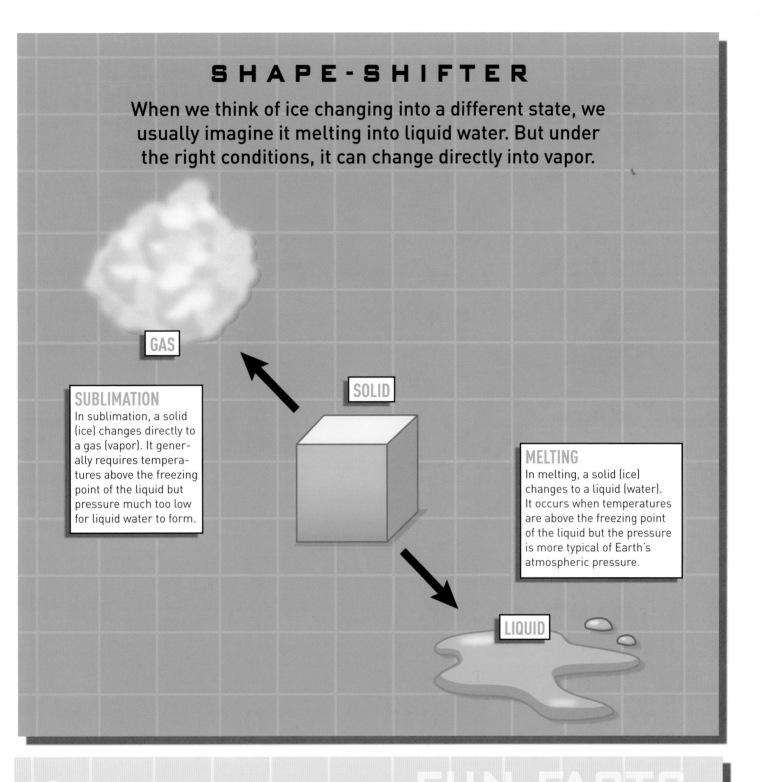

GAS

SOLID

SUBLIMATION
In sublimation, a solid (ice) changes directly to a gas (vapor). It generally requires temperatures above the freezing point of the liquid but pressure much too low for liquid water to form.

MELTING
In melting, a solid (ice) changes to a liquid (water). It occurs when temperatures are above the freezing point of the liquid but the pressure is more typical of Earth's atmospheric pressure.

LIQUID

FUN FACTS

● Under the right conditions, **snow vaporizes** instead of melting. It happens a lot on the south face of **Mount Everest.** It's so tall that the atmospheric pressure is low, but it also has **strong sunlight,** strong winds, and **cold** temperatures.

● Many **"dehydrated" foods**—including instant coffee, tea, soup, and rice—actually are **freeze-dried.**

PROFILE: Emmanuel Afoakwa

FOOD SCIENTIST

You know the scenario. You're sitting at the dinner table, and your mom surveys your plate. She does a quick inventory of what's left and looks you in the eye. Here it comes: The Lecture.

"If I've told you once, I've told you a million times," she says. "Eat. Your. CHOCOLATE!"

Wait ... what? That's not how it goes in your house?

Well, it could be—if Emmanuel Ohene Afoakwa gets his way.

Emmanuel is a food scientist, and he's working to

> ## " IF I'VE TOLD YOU ONCE, I'VE TOLD YOU A MILLION TIMES, EAT. YOUR. CHOCOLATE! "

make chocolate healthier and sweeter. (Like chocolate could get better, right?)

There's evidence that chocolate—at least, dark chocolate—has some health benefits. If it's not in a candy bar loaded with sugar (which, sorry, totally bumps it out of the "healthy" category), chocolate may help keep your heart healthy and your memory sharp. Part of its health power comes from something called "antioxidants" in cocoa beans, the source of chocolate.

But here's the thing: The steps that cocoa goes through

to become chocolate can eat away some of the antioxidants. Emmanuel and his team of scientists at the University of Ghana, in West Africa, are working to change that.

FROM COCOA TO CANDY

To become chocolate, cocoa typically goes through several steps. Farmers cut down pods from cocoa trees, then split them open to scoop out the cocoa beans, which are white or purple at this point.

The farmers stick the beans in baskets lined with banana leaves for several days so they can ferment, a natural chemical process that helps clean the beans and brings out their chocolaty flavor (and turns the beans reddish brown). Then the beans dry in the sun for about a week.

The beans, now a dark brown, are roasted for 10 to 20 minutes at a high temperature to bring out their full flavor. After this entire process, the beans' shells are removed and the cocoa is ready to be made into all types of chocolate awesomeness.

If only there were a way to keep all those healthy antioxidants! Emmanuel suspected that simple changes in the process could

produce big benefits. His team started to run experiments.

In the first experiment, they stored the cocoa pods before the fermentation step. They divided 300 pods into four groups and stored some for three, seven, or 10 days before processing. The fourth group wasn't stored at all.

In the second experiment, they roasted the beans for a longer time, 45 minutes, but at a lower temperature than usual.

Emmanuel's hunches were right. Longer storage—seven days being the best—and slower roasting were better for the cocoa beans' healthy antioxidant powers. What's more, the two changes made the cocoa even sweeter. Yes!

Emmanuel hopes his research will help farmers produce better cocoa beans. About a fourth of Ghana's population depends on income from cocoa. Candy-makers also are really interested in his work. Making chocolate more nutritious and delicious is a win-win.

As for your mom telling you to eat more chocolate ... Well, it may never go quite that far. But maybe she'll feel more comfortable letting you have the occasional sweet treat.

A SINGLE COCOA POD MAY CONTAIN **40 TO 50 BEANS.**

YOU KNOW HOW COUNTRIES PUT IMPORTANT STUFF, LIKE **PAST PRESIDENTS** AND COOL BUILDINGS, ON THEIR COINS? WELL, IN GHANA, A **COCOA POD** IS DEPICTED ON ONE OF ITS COINS.

COCOA ORIGINATED IN CENTRAL AND SOUTH AMERICA MORE THAN **5,000 YEARS AGO,** AND THE REGION STILL PRODUCES A LOT OF THE **WORLD'S COCOA**—BUT SO DOES AFRICA. GHANA IS SURPASSED ONLY BY THE CÔTE D'IVOIRE.

BELGIUM IS KNOWN FOR MAKING **INCREDIBLE CHOCOLATES.** IT'S NO SURPRISE, THEN, THAT THE BELGIAN GOVERNMENT IS **HELPING** SUPPORT EMMANUEL'S RESEARCH.

CHOCOLATE'S NOT ALONE IN CONTAINING **ANTIOXIDANTS.** MANY FOODS, INCLUDING BERRIES, BEANS, NUTS, TOMATOES, CARROTS, ORANGES, AND **LEAFY GREENS** HAVE THEM, TOO.

PUCKER UP

How does **YOGURT** get its tangy-tart creaminess?

Dig In

It's a tasty, tangy snack on the go or a perfect way to start the day. Eat it plain, plop fruit in it, top it with crunchy granola. Whatever. Yogurt can take it. After all, it's got an army of bacteria on its side—it's up for anything. Find out how yogurt is made and why we're lucky that it teems with bacteria.

Why are there bacteria in it **?**

How does milk change into yogurt **?**

Why is plain yogurt tart **?**

JUST THE FACTS

Dairy Delight

Have you ever picked up a carton of yogurt and noticed it says, "Contains live cultures?" Yikes! What's that about? They're talking about bacteria. No, not the gross kind that make you sick. These bacteria are helpful, and they have an important job to do. They help transform milk into creamy, tangy yogurt by souring it in a special way. In fact, when they give yogurt its tangy taste, they help make sure bad bacteria can't survive in the food. Yay, good bacteria!

Most yogurt comes in little tubs—either **SINGLE SERVING** or larger—but that's not the only option. Thinner yogurts are bottled as **DRINKS,** and tubes of yogurt make a fun snack.

FERMENTATION TRANSFORMATION

With the help of the right kind of bacteria, it's easy to make yogurt.

1. Milk is heated to kill bad bacteria and let some of its liquid evaporate, so it gets thicker. The high temperatures also help milk's proteins interact in a way that helps create yogurt—and not cheese.

2. After the milk cools a little, good bacteria are added. They eat the lactose sugars and produce lactic acid in a process called fermentation. The lactic acid gives yogurt its tangy flavor.

3. Fruit, flavorings, or more good bacteria, called probiotics, can be added to the yogurt.

4. The yogurt heads on its way to your favorite grocery store.

WORLDLY VIEWS

People around the world are eating **more and more yogurt,** but they like it different ways. Sample these yogurt trends.

United States: Greek yogurt is the favorite, especially with fruit and for breakfast.

Brazil: Yogurt makes a tasty breakfast, along with cereal.

France: Flavored yogurt—by itself—is a delicious dessert at the end of a meal.

Poland: Flavored yogurt is a great between-meal snack.

China: Drinkable yogurt is a preferred snack, with added probiotics for health benefits.

Turkey: Plain yogurt goes perfectly with a warm entree.

FUN FACT

MOST OF THE **YOGURT** EATEN IN THE UNITED STATES IS MADE FROM THE MILK OF COWS OR SOMETIMES SHEEP OR GOATS. BUT ELSEWHERE IN THE WORLD, YOGURT IS ALSO MADE FROM THE MILK OF **WATER BUFFALO, YAKS,** OR **CAMELS.**

Bacteria pull off their nifty yogurt-creating trick by eating the lactose sugars in heated milk and turning them into lactic acid, which sours the milk and makes it thicker. It's a process called fermentation, and it takes a controlled environment for it to happen. You can modify the cooking process—tweaking the temperature or fermentation times—to get different types of yogurt, such as Greek yogurt, or to make the yogurt tangier.

YOGURT CHAMPS

Bacteria ferment the milk, souring it and changing its proteins in a way so that it's thicker and creamier.

Lactobacillus bulgaricus bacteria (shown) feed on lactose milk sugars.

FUN FACTS

In the United States, two **types of bacteria** are used to ferment milk and create yogurt. The bacteria have awfully **impressive names** for such little creatures: *Streptococcus thermophilus* and *Lactobacillus bulgaricus*. See if you can find those listed on your yogurt container.

Yogurt gets its name from the **Turkish** word *yoğurt*, which in turn is based on an old Turkish root, *yog*, which means something like "to **curdle, condense, or thicken.**"

How Things Worked

Yogurt has a really long history, and we're going to go through every part of it. (Kidding.) Here's what you need to know. It's amazingly old. Yogurt goes back possibly as far as 5000 B.C. and, like cheese, probably was an accident at first. In a region that's now southeastern Turkey, goatherds stored milk in sheepskin or goatskin bags, where naturally occurring bacteria made it ferment in the hot weather. Even if the first yogurt was an accident, it was soon a big hit and spread throughout the region. The Roman philosopher Pliny the Elder, who lived in the first century A.D., was the first to write about the wonder, noting that some nations knew how "to thicken the milk into a substance with an agreeable acidity." Yogurt was credited not only for tasting good but also for improving the health of those who regularly ate it. As legend has it, yogurt was introduced to Europe when French King

François I, also known as "Francis of the Large Nose," suffered from terrible tummy trouble that no European doctor could cure. Suleyman the Magnificent, the sultan of the Ottoman Empire, immediately dispatched his best doctor to help his French buddy. The doctor gave King François yogurt. Yep, that's all—and it worked! Perhaps it's no surprise that ancient Indian records called yogurt and honey the "food of the gods."

CRUNCH TIME

How does POPCORN become so fluffy?

Dig In

Popcorn is a serious shape-shifter. One second, it's a hard yellow nugget. Seconds later, boom! It explodes into a fluffy white snack. Along the way, it puts on a little show, popping and flipping through the air. Why does it do all that? Is it just showing off? Read on to find out its secrets.

What makes the popping sound ?

Where does the fluffy white part come from ?

Why does popcorn jump up when it pops ?

JUST THE FACTS

So Special

Don't bother trying to pop the kernels from an ear of sweet corn. You might get a pathetic little pop but nothing close to the fluffy white goodness of real popcorn. That's because they're different kinds of corn and come from different plants! Popcorn is ideally suited for making the fluffy snack. Its kernels are more ball-shaped and have stronger hulls. In other words, they're designed to act like little pressure cookers.

Getting Steamed

When you heat a popcorn kernel, the natural moisture inside of it turns into steam, expanding in the process. (Steam takes up more space than liquid water.) But inside the hard hull, the steam has nowhere to go, so it builds up a lot of pressure. Eventually the kernel's hull can't hold it any longer, and ... POP! The hull splits, and the white starch inside it bursts out in a big fluff—often making the popcorn perform an amazing acrobatic move in the process.

A close-up of a kernel's insides after popping shows damaged cell walls.

Popcorn kernels have stronger hulls than other types of corn, so they can build up steam inside.

FUN FACT

AMERICANS TOGETHER EAT ALMOST **13 BILLION QUARTS** (14.8 BILLION LITERS) OF POPCORN EACH YEAR. THAT MEANS A TYPICAL AMERICAN EATS THREE TO FOUR SERVINGS OF POPCORN **EVERY MONTH.**

PRESSURE COOKER

A popcorn kernel is perfectly built to become your favorite snack—
or a new plant! That's right, a kernel is a seed.

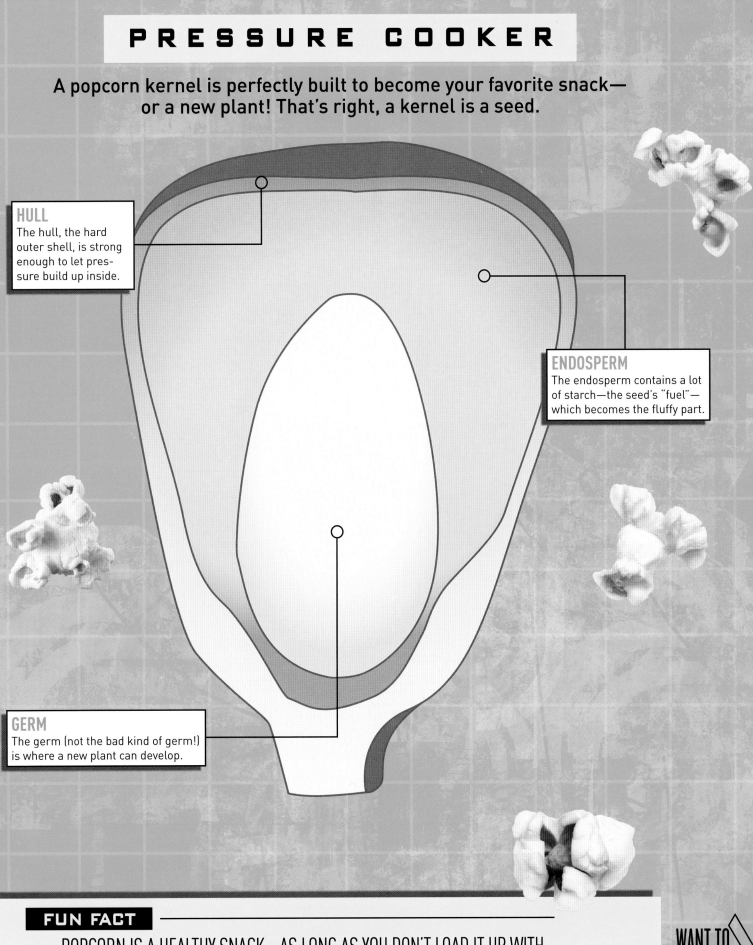

HULL
The hull, the hard outer shell, is strong enough to let pressure build up inside.

ENDOSPERM
The endosperm contains a lot of starch—the seed's "fuel"—which becomes the fluffy part.

GERM
The germ (not the bad kind of germ!) is where a new plant can develop.

FUN FACT

POPCORN IS A HEALTHY SNACK—AS LONG AS YOU DON'T LOAD IT UP WITH **A LOT OF BUTTER OR CARAMEL** COATING. IT'S A WHOLE GRAIN, LOW IN FAT, AND A GOOD SOURCE OF FIBER. **EAT UP!**

WANT TO KNOW MORE?

TELL ME MORE

There's a lot of science going on in that little kernel. When the water turns into steam, it melts the starch inside the kernel. When the kernel explodes—at about 350 degrees Fahrenheit (180 degrees Celsius)—the starch bursts out and instantly cools into a fluffy white flake. The flake hits the surface and pushes the kernel off, the same way a gymnast does, making it jump into the air and flip.

ADDING THE PERCUSSION

What makes the loud pop? You might think it's the shell cracking, but it's not. The popping noise is the sudden release of the pressurized steam. (If you've ever seen an adult open a champagne bottle with a pop, it works the same way. It's not, however, like the fizz when you open a soda bottle!) The space inside the kernel acts like a sound chamber—like the hollow part of a drum—making the pop louder.

How Things Worked

People have been chowing down on popcorn for thousands of years. Pre-Columbian indigenous peoples farmed popcorn by 5000 B.C. For most of popcorn's history, people had to pop it by holding it over some heat source. It wasn't until the 1880s that a popcorn-making machine was invented. Charles Cretors, a candy-store owner in Chicago, had created steam-powered machines to roast nuts. He adapted the machines to pop popcorn and mounted them on street carts. Popcorn gained in popularity during tough times when other treats were out of reach. It was cheap enough for people to afford during the Great Depression of the 1930s and was still available during World War II (1939 to 1945), when sugar was rationed, dealing a blow to candy lovers. In 1938, a theater owner installed popcorn machines in his theater's lobby, forever linking the crunchy snack with watching movies.

TRY THIS!

Plant breeders discovered that popcorn pops best when about 14 percent of the kernel's mass is water. This amount is just right for turning into steam. Don't believe that the hard golden kernel has so much water inside? Here's a way to see for yourself. Put about 20 kernels in a container and weigh it on a kitchen scale. (Subtract the weight of the container, which you'll have to weigh separately.) Now pop the kernels in a microwave container or air popper. Don't add anything like oil or butter. After the popcorn does its amazing transformation, weigh it again (and subtract the weight of the container). How much does that popcorn weigh now that it's dry puffs? Be a good scientist and repeat the experiment several times, so you can make sure. (We won't tell you what to do with your experiment's results. We bet you can figure something out. Yum.)

For thousands of years, people have made popcorn over a heat source.

POPCORN ACROBATICS

Mystery solved! It's not the burst of steam that sends the popcorn shooting into the air, it's the fluffy flakes. They burst out and kick off the surface, like gymnasts do with their legs.

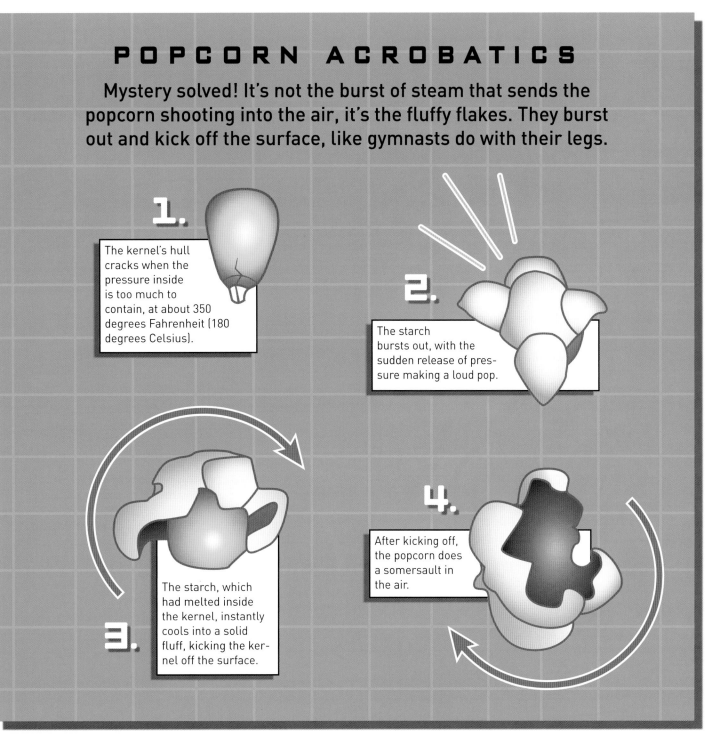

1. The kernel's hull cracks when the pressure inside is too much to contain, at about 350 degrees Fahrenheit (180 degrees Celsius).

2. The starch bursts out, with the sudden release of pressure making a loud pop.

3. The starch, which had melted inside the kernel, instantly cools into a solid fluff, kicking the kernel off the surface.

4. After kicking off, the popcorn does a somersault in the air.

FUN FACTS

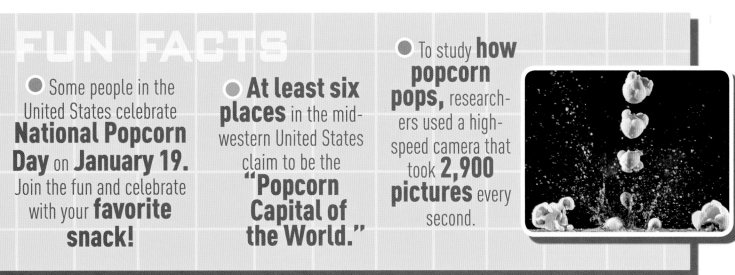

- Some people in the United States celebrate **National Popcorn Day** on **January 19.** Join the fun and celebrate with your **favorite snack!**

- **At least six places** in the midwestern United States claim to be the **"Popcorn Capital of the World."**

- To study **how popcorn pops,** researchers used a high-speed camera that took **2,900 pictures** every second.

TALES FROM THE LAB

HYBRID FRUIT:
CREATING THE PLUMCOT

You may never have heard of a plumcot. They go by different names, and some grocery stores just lump them in with plums and label them that way—even though that's not accurate. But whatever you call it, there's no denying that the plumcot is one of nature's sweetest treats.

Like plums, plumcots grow on trees. But they didn't start out that way.

The juicy summer fruit was the brainchild of plant breeders. They didn't find a plumcot tree—they created it. The fruit's name gives away their secret: They bred a plum and an apricot and created a hybrid fruit.

> **IT TOOK THE HOPEFUL PLANT BREEDERS MORE THAN A CENTURY.**

Hybrid?! Does that mean it's "Franken-fruit"? Nope. The plumcot wasn't created in a laboratory. But it was created with science: plant genetics. Two different, but related, kinds of plants were crossbred to produce a brand-new plant with the best traits of both parents.

To grow the hybrid fruit, the plant breeders acted like bees. As bees buzz from one plant to another, they transfer pollen—the tiny, powdery grains that help plants reproduce—from one flower to another. If the pollen gets to the right spot in a flower, it grows a seed and fruit. The plant breeders did the bee part, transferring apricot pollen to a plum plant (and vice versa).

Bees pollinate in a matter of minutes, but it took the hopeful plant breeders more than a century to create today's plumcot.

FIRST TRY
In the late 1800s and early 1900s, Luther Burbank, the "plant wizard," was experimenting with plums. He wondered if he could add some apricot traits to create a fruit that wouldn't bruise as easily as most plums.

"It was like entering an unexplored country," he wrote. "Apricot flowers were dusted with plum pollen and plum flowers with apricot pollen. But for a long time the experiment failed. Finally, however, when I about despaired of success, several cross-bred seedlings were found."

It felt like a miracle to him. He had created plumcots, hybrid fruit that was sweet but firm enough to handle a few bumps on the way to the market. There was just one problem: Luther's plumcot trees were hard to grow. They required too much care to thrive on their own in an orchard, so they never really caught on.

But that changed nearly a century later.

SUCCESS
Floyd Zaiger, a master at creating new types of fruit, knew Luther's work, and believed it was possible to create a plum-apricot hybrid that fruit lovers would want to eat—and orchards would want to grow. He got to work.

In the 1980s, Floyd's company, Zaiger Genetics, produced its own plumcot. The fruit was even tastier than Luther's early version, but the tree was still hard to grow.

Floyd didn't give up. His company kept experimenting, creating increasingly complex hybrids. In 1990, he found the magic formula: a plumcot-plum cross that produced a sweet, juicy fruit that's a bit more plum than apricot—and a tree that grows easily.

To escape the plumcot tree's troublesome reputation, Floyd called his creation a "pluot"—and he trademarked the name, so only Zaiger hybrids could use it. Zaiger Genetics went on to create many pluot varieties, and other plant breeders followed suit, some calling their fruit plumcots, others using entirely different names.

Whatever you call them, these sweet hybrid fruits are now widely available and even more popular than their parents.

THE **NAMES OF PLUOT VARIETIES** ARE AS CREATIVE AS THE FRUIT ITSELF. CHECK YOUR **LOCAL MARKET** FOR DAPPLE DANDY, FALL FIESTA, HONEY PUNCH, RUBY KAT, AND DINOSAUR EGGS.

Luther Burbank, the "plant wizard"

LUTHER BURBANK CREATED MORE THAN **800 NEW PLANTS.** HIS MOST FAMOUS WERE A TYPE OF **PLUM,** A HEARTY **POTATO,** AND THE **SHASTA DAISY.**

plumcot

WHEN FLOYD ZAIGER FIRST STARTED TO GROW **HYBRID PLANTS,** HE AND HIS WIFE, BETTY, WOULD PLANT SEEDLINGS AT NIGHT WITH THE **LIGHT OF A FULL MOON** BECAUSE THEY COULDN'T TAKE TIME AWAY FROM THEIR DAY JOBS.

PLUMCOTS HAVE BEEN FOUND **GROWING ON THEIR OWN** IN REGIONS OF THE WORLD WHERE BOTH PLUMS AND APRICOTS GROW.

Make It BETTER!

Pluots aren't the only hybrid fruits that Zaiger Genetics created. If you'd prefer a more apricot-y than plummy hybrid, try an aprium. Or perhaps you're more a fan of peaches? In that case, the peacotum, a complex apricot-plum-peach hybrid, may be perfect. How about a plum-size cherry? You can get pretty close with a pluerry.

Some plant breeders have crossed grapefruits and tangerines to create tangelos, Key limes and kumquats to produce limequats, and different varieties of strawberries to produce pineberries with a slight pineapple flavor.

If these juicy creations don't get your mouth watering, why not come up with your own hybrid fruit? If you were a plant scientist, which plants would you crossbreed, and what would you call your creation? Remember, in plant genetics, you can't crossbreed plants that are way too different. So, probably no bananaberries. (*Noooo!*) But a nectarcherry? That might be something to sink your teeth into!

LET IT FLOW

How does MELTED CHEESE become so gooey?

Dig In

Nothing's better than biting into a toasty pizza topped with ooey-gooey, stretchy cheese. But you can't throw any old cheese on top of a crust and expect pizza perfection. Only some cheeses melt in a way worthy of the pies. Others just become chunky, puddled messes. Want to know why? Read on to learn what makes a perfect pizza topper.

Which kinds of cheese melt **?**

What happens when cheese melts **?**

Does processed cheese product melt **?**

JUST THE FACTS

Curds and Whey

Ever wonder what in the world Little Miss Muffet was eating? What exactly is whey? Here's a cheesy answer.

Cheese—like yogurt, butter, and ice cream—starts off as milk. To become cheese, the milk first has to go sour and then become lumpy, or curdle. Cheesemakers add lemon juice, vinegar, or rennet, an enzyme (a type of protein that speeds up reactions), to make the milk curdle. While the creamy curds form, a liquid called … you guessed it … whey drips off. The curdling step (and what you do after that) affects what kind of cheese you get—and how it melts.

Melting—Kind Of

If you want to get technical, cheese doesn't really melt. True melting is when a solid turns into a liquid, like ice to water. When you heat cheese, it gets soft and gooey, but it doesn't change from one state of matter to another. If you looked inside cheese at its protein molecules—the smallest bits that make the protein—you'd see an amazing change. Most of the time, the protein molecules hold all the cheese parts, including the fats and water inside, firmly in place. But when you heat it up, the protein molecules become flexible, letting the cheese flow into the gooey stringiness we love.

INTERNATIONAL FLAVORS

Melted cheese is a star in **many traditional dishes, especially in Europe and the Americas. Take this tasty tour.**

Khachapuri:
Toasty flatbread stuffed with a tangy local cheese is a favorite treat in the country of Georgia, which borders the Black Sea.

Pizza:
It may be popular worldwide, but we have Naples, Italy, to thank for the savory pie. Melted cheese on a tasty crust is only the beginning for this dish, which can be loaded with different toppings.

Pupusa:
In this traditional Salvadoran dish, a thick corn tortilla is stuffed with fillings, often one or more cheeses, and grilled.

Croque monsieur:
This is no ordinary grilled cheese sandwich! The French cover a ham-and-cheese sandwich in a cheesy sauce for an extra-rich meal.

Queso fundido:
A mix of Mexican cheeses are melted on a hot iron or in a clay pot until they bubble and steam, and then scooped into tortillas to eat.

Saganaki:
In this Greek appetizer, cheese is fried until bubbly—sometimes set on fire in a showy display—and drenched with lemon juice.

Pão de queijo:
These cheese puffs, which have a crispy outside and warm, melted cheese inside, are popular for snacks or even breakfast in Brazil.

Pierogi:
The national dish of Poland, these dumplings can have various stuffings, but farmer's cheese is a tasty classic. The dumplings often are topped with sour cream.

Fondue:
Switzerland's national dish consists of cheeses melted in a pot with wine and other seasonings. You dip bread, veggies, or meats into the bubbling fondue.

FUN FACT
MELTED CHEESE **NEVER BECAME PART** OF THE TRADITIONAL DIETS IN **CHINESE, EAST ASIAN, AND AFRICAN** COOKING. HILLY ASIAN TERRAIN AND COMPACT LIVING DIDN'T LEAVE ROOM FOR MILK-PRODUCING COWS AND GOATS. SOME **AFRICAN CUISINE** INCLUDES MILK PRODUCTS—BUT MORE OFTEN YOGURT OR FRESH CHEESE CURDS.

SAY CHEESE!

To transform milk into cheese takes several steps. Two important steps affect whether you'll end up with a good-melting cheese.

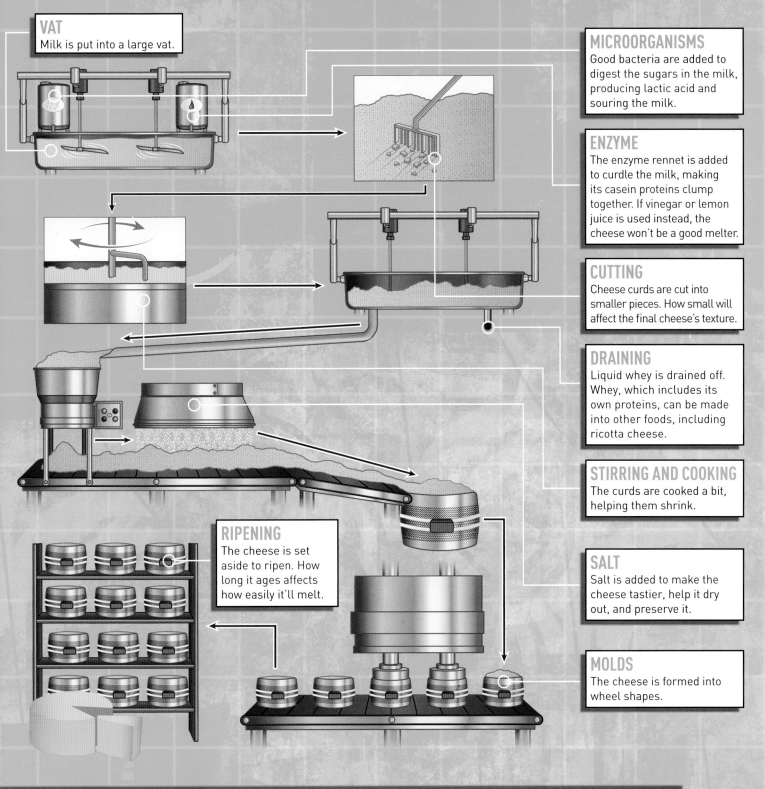

VAT
Milk is put into a large vat.

MICROORGANISMS
Good bacteria are added to digest the sugars in the milk, producing lactic acid and souring the milk.

ENZYME
The enzyme rennet is added to curdle the milk, making its casein proteins clump together. If vinegar or lemon juice is used instead, the cheese won't be a good melter.

CUTTING
Cheese curds are cut into smaller pieces. How small will affect the final cheese's texture.

DRAINING
Liquid whey is drained off. Whey, which includes its own proteins, can be made into other foods, including ricotta cheese.

STIRRING AND COOKING
The curds are cooked a bit, helping them shrink.

SALT
Salt is added to make the cheese tastier, help it dry out, and preserve it.

MOLDS
The cheese is formed into wheel shapes.

RIPENING
The cheese is set aside to ripen. How long it ages affects how easily it'll melt.

FUN FACT
LEGEND HAS IT THAT A SHEPHERD IN THE MIDDLE EAST **ACCIDENTALLY** MADE THE **FIRST CHEESE** AS FAR BACK AS **8000** B.C. UNDER THE HOT SUN, THE ENZYMES LINING A SHEEP-STOMACH BAG CURDLED THE MILK HE WAS CARRYING. AT THE END OF THE DAY, HE WAS SURPRISED TO DISCOVER CHEESE CURDS AND WHEY.

WANT TO KNOW MORE?

TELL ME MORE

Some cheeses melt into a bubbly flow of molten deliciousness. Others don't melt at all. They may just get chunky and squirt out an oily mess. How easily a cheese melts depends mostly on how its proteins are holding together. The main protein in cheese is called casein. When cheese is curdled with lemon juice or vinegar, the casein proteins link too tightly to break apart—even when heated. But when rennet is used, the bonds between casein proteins are looser and can break apart when the cheese is heated. How long a cheese is aged also matters. When a cheese is first formed, the casein proteins hold together in a flexible web, but over time the bonds hold tighter and tighter. The older the cheese, the harder it is to melt.

Myth vs. FACT

MYTH: Processed American cheese food—those single slices of cheese wrapped in plastic—won't melt because the stuff isn't "real" cheese.

FACT: A video making the rounds on the Internet showed someone trying to melt a single slice of processed American cheese over a flame. (This isn't a smart way to melt cheese—don't try it.) When it didn't melt, social media went crazy. People wondered what was up, why wouldn't the American cheese melt, was it EVEN REAL? Processed American cheese (also called "process cheese product" or "cheese food") contains real cheese, but it's not 100 percent cheese. (It, however, must contain at least 51 percent cheese.) The processed product is made by taking cheeses and blending them together with other ingredients, including substances called emulsifiers, which help bind the fats and proteins together. The result is a supersmooth, convenient product that doesn't spoil easily. Some people don't like the fact that it's not 100 percent cheese or has emulsifiers and other things added to it. But you can't claim it won't melt! One of processed American cheese slice's claims to fame is how smoothly and evenly it melts. It's a star in many grilled cheese sandwiches.

FUN FACTS

- Most cheeses that Americans eat are made from cow milk (**cheddar, Swiss, Parmesan,** and many more) or sheep milk (**feta, Pecorino Romano,** and others).

- You might think that **Italians,** with their pizzas and pastas, eat more cheese than anyone else. But the gold medal actually **goes to Denmark,** where a typical person eats **61.95 pounds** (28.1 kg) of cheese every year. The average American eats about 36.8 pounds (16.7 kg) of cheese annually.

HANGING OUT

How a cheese is curdled affects how strongly its casein proteins hang together—and whether it'll melt.

RENNET ADDED

LEMON JUICE ADDED

RENNET
When the enzyme rennet is used to make the cheese curdle, like for cheddar or mozzarella, the casein proteins link together like a web, holding the fats and water inside.

ACID
When lemon juice or vinegar is used to make the cheese curdle, like for cottage cheese, the casein proteins link together tightly in clumps, squeezing out the water.

When heated, the casein proteins loosen their hold on one another and flow out with the fats, which have melted into liquids. Great melting action!

When heated, the casein proteins stay clumped together, but the fat puddles separately. Not a great melter!

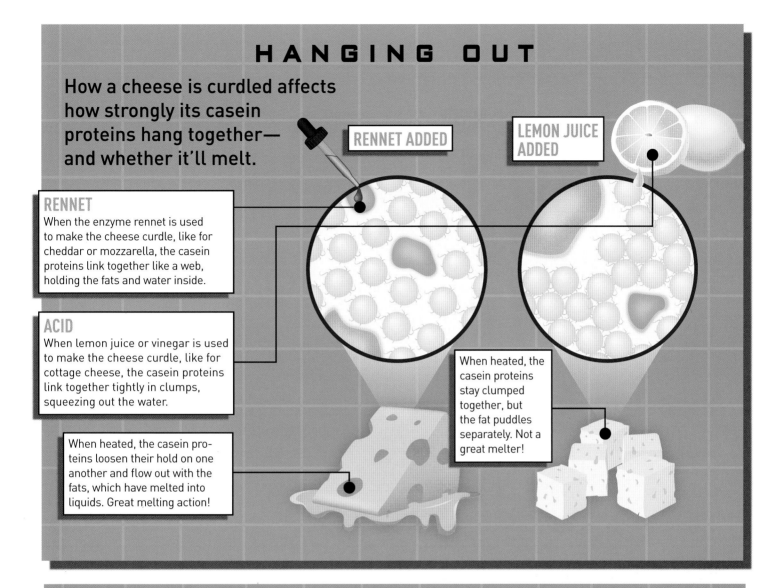

YOUNG AND OLD

The aging process changes how tightly a cheese's casein proteins hold together—and how well the cheese melts.

YOUNG
In young cheeses, the web of protein bonds is not as strong. The flexibility lets them break and flow out with the melted fats.

AGED
In aged cheeses, the casein proteins bond tighter and tighter. The fats melt long before the protein bonds give way—giving you clumps and puddles.

ALL SPUN UP

How is COTTON CANDY made?

Dig In

Few things scream "carnival" as much as cotton candy. Just the thought of a freshly spun, airy cloud of still warm sweetness can make your mouth start to water. Have you ever wondered how it's made—or why it melts the second it makes contact with your tongue? Read on to learn about this sweet treat.

What's the "cotton" made of ?

How does it get so puffy ?

Why is it so sweet ?

JUST THE FACTS

Sugar Spinner

There's a very good reason cotton candy is so sweet. It's sugar. Period. End of explanation. OK, OK, there's more to it than that, of course.

Cotton candy goes through an amazing change to become your favorite fluffy treat.

Inside a cotton-candy machine, grains of sugar are melted into a liquid, which is forced through little holes as the machine spins. The thin strands of melted sugar—no thicker than one of your hairs—cool instantly when they hit the air. They're ready to be twirled together for a melt-in-your-mouth treat.

COTTON CREATOR

It doesn't take many ingredients to make cotton candy, and a handy machine does the hard work.

You pour granulated sugar (usually tinted with food coloring) into the center of the spinning device.

Inside the spinning device, heating elements—kind of like the coils inside your toaster—heat the sugar, turning it into a liquid.

The sugar strands cool the instant they hit the air.

As the device spins, centrifugal force pushes the molten sugar out the holes in the center.

The sticky strands cling to each other, so they're easy to roll into a puffy cloud.

In China, cotton candy is an **ART FORM.** Some cotton-candy makers sculpt multicolored **"FLOWERS"** the size of umbrellas by layering different colors of cotton candy. Move over, Willy Wonka.

TELL ME MORE

CHANGE ARTIST

Sugar does an amazing shape-shifting trick to become cotton candy. It starts as solid, grainlike crystals, melts into a liquid, and then reforms as solid, flexible strands. To understand what's going on, let's peek at sugar's molecules, the tiniest bits that make sucrose (table sugar's scientific name). At room temperature, the molecules hold on to their neighbors, keeping the sucrose in its solid, crystal form. But when you warm it up, the heat energy makes the molecules jiggle a lot, much more than when they're cool. Some break away from their neighbors and find new molecule friends. Others actually break apart and form different molecules. The sugar doesn't only turn to liquid, it turns into caramel. When the intense heat's gone, the molecules slow down and regroup—this time in strands.

FUN FACTS

● Talk about a sweet tooth! A Turkish group that puts on fairs and carnivals created a **4,593-foot** (1,400-m)-long cotton candy in 2009. The sweet weighed 661 pounds (300 kg) and took **70 staff members six hours** to make. A German group went up instead of long. They made a nearly **18-foot** (5.45-m)-tall treat in 2013.

● The first cotton-candy machines were **invented by dentists.** Yes, you read that correctly. The machines for making sugary treats that stick to your teeth were invented by dentists. Maybe they needed **more patients?**

How Things Worked

Lots of people want to get credit for inventing cotton candy! It may go back as far as the 15th century in Italy. What's known for sure is that sugar was an expensive treat, enjoyed only by rich people back in the Middle Ages. Cooks would melt sugar and spin it around on forks and then use the spun sugar to decorate cakes. (Even today, cooks make some amazing creations from melted sugar.) In the late 1890s, two inventors received a patent for the first "machine that melted and spun sugar." They took their invention to the 1904 World's Fair in St. Louis and delighted fairgoers with the treats. They sold 69,000 boxes for 25 cents a piece—a good chunk of change back then. They earned more than $17,000, which would be like half a million dollars today.

TRY THIS!

You really need a cotton-candy machine to make the fluffy stuff. (Sorry.) But here's another sweet experiment that'll give you a close look at sugar crystals. Grab a grown-up to help because this experiment is a hot one. Boil about 1 1/2 cups (400 ml) of water in a clean pot and add about 3/4 cup (200 ml) of sugar to the water. Stir it really well so all the sugar dissolves. Pour the sugar solution into a clean jar, preferably glass, that can handle the heat. Take a clean, cotton string and tie one end around the middle of a pencil (or something else that's long enough to bridge the top of the jar). Put the pencil across the top of the jar, and stick the long end of the string into your sugar solution. Try to make the string as straight as possible, but don't sweat it too much. Put the jar somewhere safe and keep checking it over the next several days. It takes a while—maybe a week—but sugar crystals should grow on the string. And, yes, you can eat the rock candy. Sweet!

TRY THIS!

SNACK SCIENCE

WHIP UP A BATCH OF VANILLA MERINGUE COOKIES

You can eat eggs in many forms, but nothing beats the fun of beating egg whites into stiff peaks and then baking them into crispy, airy meringue cookies. Put on your chef's hat and head to the kitchen. It's time to conduct a scientific experiment that has melt-in-your-mouth results.

WHAT YOU NEED

TIME: about half an hour of active preparation, plus an hour break in the middle, an hour to bake, and more cooling-down time

A grown-up to help get things into the hot oven

1. 3 large eggs, chilled (like from the fridge)
2. 1 1/2 teaspoons (7 ml) of vanilla extract
3. 1/4 teaspoon (1.25 ml) cream of tartar
4. A dash of salt
5. 2/3 cup (227 g) of sugar
6. Large mixing bowl, preferably glass (clean and dry)
7. Drinking Glass
8. Measuring spoons
9. Mixer (hand or stand)
10. Parchment paper
11. Baking sheets (aka cookie sheets)
12. Oven
13. Oven mitts
14. Spoon
15. Pastry bag or food-safe plastic bag (optional)
16. Fancy pastry tip, like a star tip (optional)

WHAT TO DO

1. WASH YOUR HANDS. (Always a good first step for chefs and scientists.)

2. PUT A SHEET of parchment paper on your baking sheets.

3. YOU'LL NEED TO "SEPARATE" the eggs. (What?!) Relax, here's an easy way to do it. Tap the middle of an egg on the edge of a glass to crack open its shell. Open up the egg over your bowl, keeping the yellow yolk inside one of the shell halves but letting the gooey, clear egg white drip into the bowl. Gently pour the yolk into the other shell half, letting more white drip into the bowl. Go back and forth between the two shell halves a couple of times so all the white drips down. Don't let any of the yellow yolk into the bowl! (If it accidentally happens, start over.) Repeat with the rest of the eggs. (Tip: This is the trickiest step. We won't judge you if you ask a parent for help.)

4. THROW AWAY the egg shells. Either pitch the yolks, too, or keep them in the 'fridge to cook later. You only need the egg whites for this recipe.

5. WASH YOUR HANDS again to remove all the egg.

6. LET THE EGG WHITES sit in the small bowl on a counter for 30 minutes to an hour or so, until they're room temperature. (Yes, it's hard to wait, but your patience will be rewarded. Trust us!)

7. PREHEAT YOUR OVEN to 250 degrees Fahrenheit (120 degrees Celsius).

8. ADD YOUR VANILLA, cream of tartar, and salt to the bowl of egg whites. Beat with a mixer with clean, dry beaters at medium speed until the egg whites get foamy and form soft peaks if you stop your beaters and pull them up.

9. GRADUALLY ADD the sugar, a spoonful at a time, and beat at a high speed after each addition until all the sugar is dissolved and still, glossy peaks form. It'll take about seven, maybe up to 10 minutes. (Tip: You want to make sure the peaks stand tall on their own and don't curl over. But don't overdo it. If they get too stiff, they'll break.)

10. OPTIONAL: If you want to make fancy-shmancy cookies, cut a small hole in your pastry bag or the corner of a food-safe plastic bag and insert the fancy tip. Spoon the meringue batter into the bag. Twist the top of the bag closed, then squeeze out little mounds of meringue (about 1 1/4 inch, or 3 cm, across) onto the baking sheet. Space them out a bit, about 2 inches (5 cm) apart so they have room to puff up when they bake.

11. IF YOU DON'T HAVE a pastry bag and fancy tip, scoop the batter with a spoon and drop each little mound onto the baking sheet. (It's OK if you need to use a finger to help—just wash again.) You'll have about 50 mounds. They won't look as fancy, but they'll be just as delicious.

12. ASK YOUR GROWN-UP to put the baking sheets into the hot oven.

13. BAKE THE COOKIES FOR about an hour, so they're firm to the touch but not turning brown. Here's another tricky part: You can't open the door to touch them! Get a second opinion if you're not sure they look firm. Once you're pretty sure they're done baking, turn off the oven. Leave the cookies inside the oven for another hour or two until they're dry all the way. (Longer doesn't hurt. Some people leave them overnight!)

14. TAKE THE COOL COOKIES on the cool baking sheets out of the cool oven. (If anything isn't cool yet, you need to wait longer.) Remove them from the baking sheets and store them in an airtight container at room temperature.

15. TASTE YOUR CREATION! Share them!

NINE CHEFS FROM THE TOWN OF GRUYÈRES, SWITZERLAND, MADE A RECORD-LONG MERINGUE IN 2016. MEASURING IN AT 328 FEET (100 M) LONG—ABOUT THE LENGTH OF A FOOTBALL FIELD—IT USED 1,000 EGG WHITES.

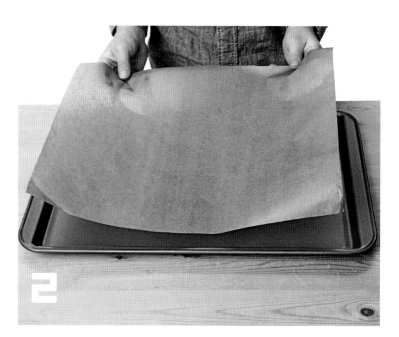

8

DESPITE ITS NAME, CREAM OF TARTAR ISN'T CREAMY. IT'S A DRY POWDER—AND IT HAS ABSOLUTELY NOTHING TO DO WITH THE GUNK THAT BUILDS UP ON TEETH. IT'S ACTUALLY PRODUCED AS PART OF THE PROCESS OF TURNING GRAPES INTO WINE.

9

WHAT TO EXPECT

Light, airy, crispy deliciousness.

WHAT'S GOING ON?

When you beat egg whites, you mix air (a gas) into the liquid and create foam. Foam is just a bunch of little bubbles, each with air inside. The egg white spreads out into a thin film to hold the bubbles together and support them, eventually into peaks. If you tried to beat plain old water, you'd get some bubbles but they wouldn't last. But egg whites contain a team of proteins, which pull off a cool trick. Usually the proteins are folded and curled up in little tangles (too small to see) inside the egg white. But when you beat them, the proteins uncurl and stretch out, bonding to each other and making firm walls for the foam. Baking the meringue evaporates the water from inside it—and it's the reason you leave the oven door shut. You don't want any moisture from humid, outside air to sneak into the oven.

CHAPTER 5

LIGHTS, CAMERA ... ACTION!

HOORAY FOR HOLLYWOOD!

Talk about transporting us to other worlds—few things do that better than a great movie. It's not only great acting and stunt work that bring a story to life on the big screen. There's a lot of behind-the-scenes wizardry, too. High-tech filming, projection, and sound systems immerse us in the movie world. And the special effects? Whoa! Animatronics make dinosaurs roar, sound artists make us dodge laser blasts, and animators create fantastical beasts that we'd swear are real. So grab some popcorn! We're going to the movies. Action!

SHOW TIME!

How do MOVIE CAMERAS and PROJECTORS work their cinematic magic?

Dig In

Capturing a story world and re-creating it on the big screen takes talent and technology. How the movie is shot and how it's shown determine how real it feels to us. It's not only a question of film quality. Moviemakers also use specific movie cameras and formats to create moods to fit the story—and they rely on projectors to transfer their vision to the big screen. Step behind the scenes and see how movie tech makes our viewing experience real.

How does a movie camera work ?

Does it shoot film or digital images ?

How do projectors show movies ?

JUST THE FACTS

Flipping Photos

Movies are like high-tech flip books—in which each page has a picture that's slightly different from the next. When you flip the pictures fast, they look like they're moving. For movies, the pictures are captured on frames of film or recorded digitally as electronic signals instead of on paper. When we watch a movie, we don't see each individual frame, of course. The frames move fast enough through the projector that they look like continuous movement.

Decisions, Decisions

Just like their cousins that shoot still images, movie cameras can shoot either film or digital. Since 2012, more big movies have been shot using digital cameras. Directors like how the crisp digital images can be tweaked after they're shot—and how easy it is to distribute them to theaters. But plenty of big-name movie directors prefer the more traditional look of film, which they think has more realistic colors and makes people look more attractive. It's a trade-off.

SIZE MATTERS

When directors shoot a movie on film, they need to **pick a film format** to match their vision—and their budget. Bigger films capture more detail and produce a better picture, but they cost more. Here are what common formats offer.

16mm:
The smallest and cheapest format—not often used in blockbusters—its quality gives films a rough look.

16mm

35mm:
The traditional format used by most movies shot on film—almost all of them before 2008—but still used today.

35mm

VistaVision:
A 35mm film turned sideways so each image is 65 percent larger.

VistaVision

65mm:
A big, expensive film, used when movies will go to IMAX screens—or when the director is famous enough to get the money to use it.

65mm

70mm:
This large format, used for IMAX films, delivers the clearest, crispest colors.

70mm

FUN FACT

THE 2014 **BLOCKBUSTER MOVIE** *INTERSTELLAR*, WHICH WAS A WHOPPING 2 HOURS AND 47 MINUTES LONG, USED SO MUCH IMAX FILM THAT IT **TOOK A FORKLIFT** TO MOVE THE 600-POUND (272-KG) FILM REEL.

THAT'S A WRAP!

A basic film movie camera captures individual images—24 per second or more—on a long roll of film that moves from one reel to another.

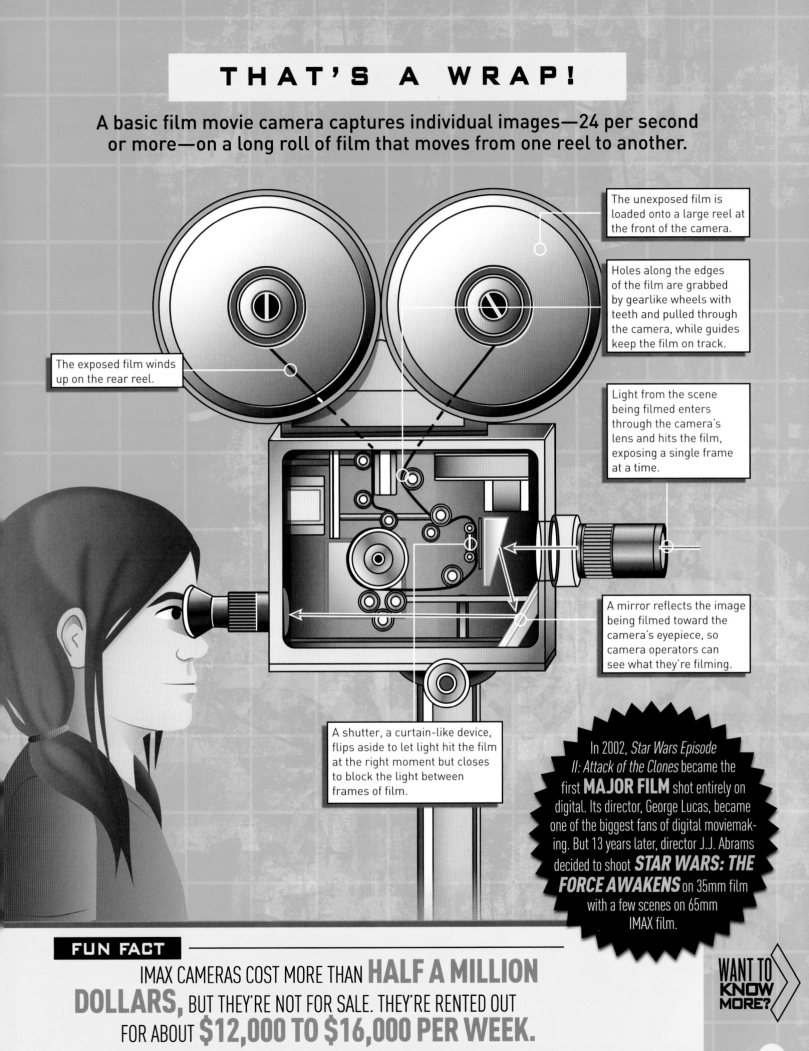

The unexposed film is loaded onto a large reel at the front of the camera.

Holes along the edges of the film are grabbed by gearlike wheels with teeth and pulled through the camera, while guides keep the film on track.

The exposed film winds up on the rear reel.

Light from the scene being filmed enters through the camera's lens and hits the film, exposing a single frame at a time.

A mirror reflects the image being filmed toward the camera's eyepiece, so camera operators can see what they're filming.

A shutter, a curtain-like device, flips aside to let light hit the film at the right moment but closes to block the light between frames of film.

In 2002, *Star Wars Episode II: Attack of the Clones* became the first **MAJOR FILM** shot entirely on digital. Its director, George Lucas, became one of the biggest fans of digital moviemaking. But 13 years later, director J.J. Abrams decided to shoot ***STAR WARS: THE FORCE AWAKENS*** on 35mm film with a few scenes on 65mm IMAX film.

FUN FACT

IMAX CAMERAS COST MORE THAN **HALF A MILLION DOLLARS,** BUT THEY'RE NOT FOR SALE. THEY'RE RENTED OUT FOR ABOUT **$12,000 TO $16,000 PER WEEK.**

WANT TO KNOW MORE?

TELL ME MORE

MAKING IT REAL

The best movie cameras capture great detail and vibrant colors. It's a shame we may not see it all! Traditional movie projectors with bulbs don't even get as bright as most televisions. (Televisions have their own issues: They don't show the entire range of colors captured in a movie.) But movie theaters are switching to new projection systems with lasers, so they can show movies with true-to-life colors and as the director meant for them to be seen.

WHOA ... SLOW DOWN!
A Closer Look at Image Quality

When people talk about the quality of an image, they can use a lot of jargon. "Contrast" and "saturation" are two common terms—and important to know. Let's take a look at what they mean. Contrast is easiest to understand if you think about the extremes: black and white. It's the difference between the darkest, absolute black and pure white. It's actually hard to get good contrast out of projectors—and even some TV sets. If you brighten a picture to get pure whites, you might lose pure blacks. You also might lose some of the color saturation. Saturation refers to how intense a color is. You can think of it as how strong the color is and also how pure it is. You want yellow to be bright—but not because some white got mixed in and lightened it up. You want pure, bold yellow, like you'd see in real life.

ROLL THE FILM!

Like a flip book, a projector shows a series of still images in quick succession to give a sense of movement.

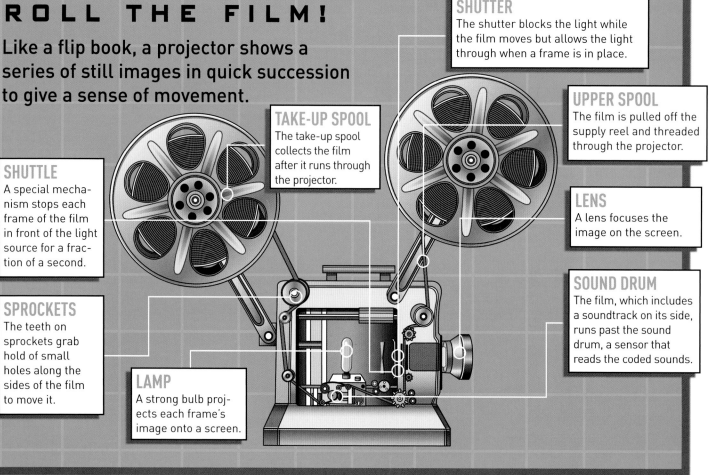

SHUTTER
The shutter blocks the light while the film moves but allows the light through when a frame is in place.

UPPER SPOOL
The film is pulled off the supply reel and threaded through the projector.

TAKE-UP SPOOL
The take-up spool collects the film after it runs through the projector.

SHUTTLE
A special mechanism stops each frame of the film in front of the light source for a fraction of a second.

LENS
A lens focuses the image on the screen.

SOUND DRUM
The film, which includes a soundtrack on its side, runs past the sound drum, a sensor that reads the coded sounds.

SPROCKETS
The teeth on sprockets grab hold of small holes along the sides of the film to move it.

LAMP
A strong bulb projects each frame's image onto a screen.

LIGHT SHOW

Laser projectors produce more intense colors and in a wider range than bulb projectors.

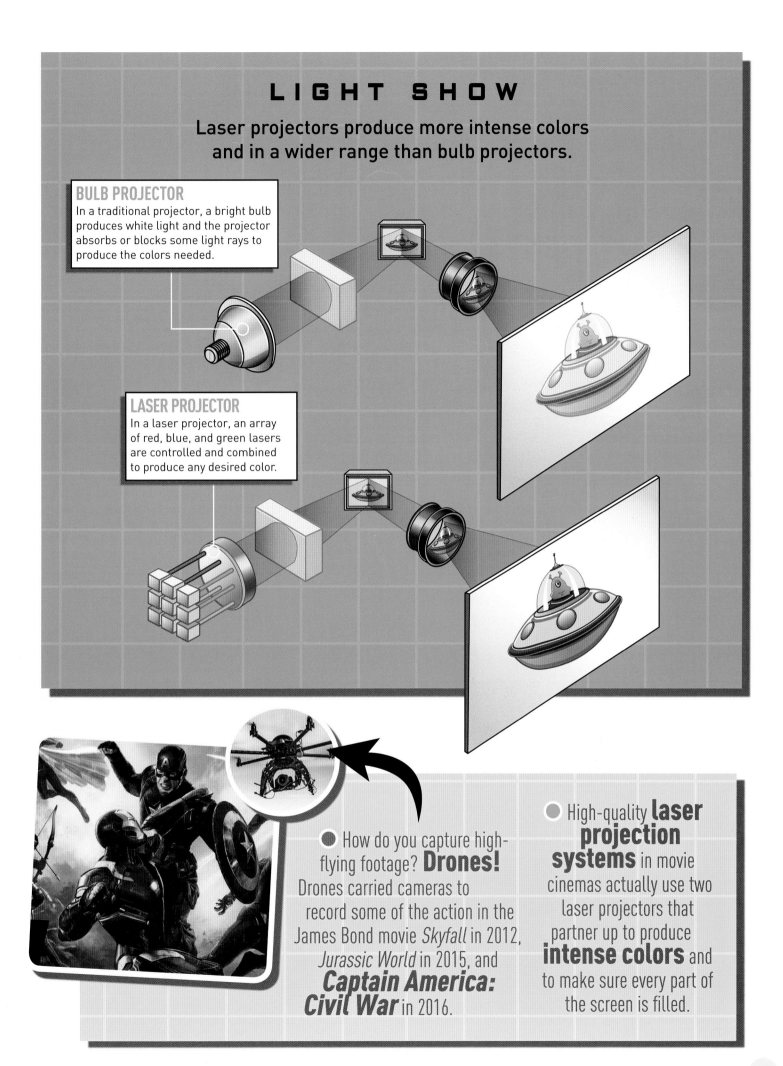

BULB PROJECTOR
In a traditional projector, a bright bulb produces white light and the projector absorbs or blocks some light rays to produce the colors needed.

LASER PROJECTOR
In a laser projector, an array of red, blue, and green lasers are controlled and combined to produce any desired color.

● How do you capture high-flying footage? **Drones!** Drones carried cameras to record some of the action in the James Bond movie *Skyfall* in 2012, *Jurassic World* in 2015, and ***Captain America: Civil War*** in 2016.

● High-quality **laser projection systems** in movie cinemas actually use two laser projectors that partner up to produce **intense colors** and to make sure every part of the screen is filled.

SOUND BYTES

How does SURROUND SOUND work?

Dig In

You can learn a lot about what's happening around you just by listening. (But, no, not by eavesdropping on your parents.) Pay attention to the sounds around you. Did a car drive by? Which direction was it heading? Is your sibling trying to sneak up on you from behind? Moviemakers want to make the movie experience as real as possible—well, maybe not the sneaky sibling part. But they do want us to sense movement through the theater, and they can engineer movie sounds to make that happen. Read on to learn how they do it.

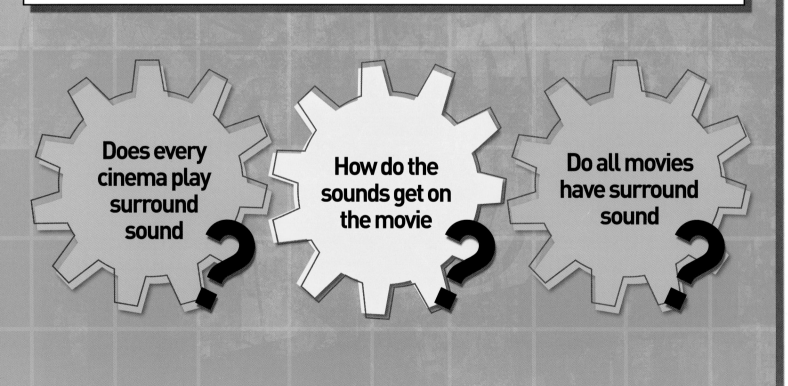

Does every cinema play surround sound?

How do the sounds get on the movie?

Do all movies have surround sound?

JUST THE FACTS

Making All the Right Noises

One of the ways moviemakers immerse you in the movie world is through the movie theater's sound system. Theaters use multiple speakers—usually six to 10—that trick you into thinking you're completely surrounded by sound. A speaker in the center-front handles most of the dialogue, while speakers on the sides (front and back) play the rest of the sounds. By fading the sound from one speaker while strengthening it on another—a technique called panning—movies create the sense of movement, so you feel like a jet soars over your head when its sound moves from the front speakers to the rear. An additional speaker called a subwoofer, which plays really low sounds, adds the booms of explosions and rumbles of earthquakes.

Capturing the Sound

It might seem like it takes a really incredible microphone to record surround sound, but it doesn't. Sound technicians don't actually record surround sound on set. They create the surround soundtracks in the studio. Sound editors and engineers take multiple audio recordings—actors' dialogue recorded on set, sound effects and music recorded in studios—and divide them among the different sound channels that will stream to individual speakers.

SOUND SETUP

Multiple speakers in a movie theater immerse you in sound and even create the sense that things on the screen move around the theater. Even home "theaters" use surround sound systems.

Most of the actors' dialogue plays through speakers in the front-center, near where you see the actors.

Multiple side speakers from front to back handle the rest of the sound. When a sound fades in one speaker and builds up in another, it sounds like it moves around the theater. Moviemakers use that technique to make jets and spacecraft soar over your head or horses gallop from one side to another.

A subwoofer pounds out deep rumbling sounds—strong enough for you to feel—to add the bang for explosions or earthquakes.

FUN FACT

THE MOVIE *WALL-E* STANDS OUT FOR ITS EXCELLENT **SURROUND SOUND.** IN A SCENE WHERE WALL-E AND HIS GIRLFRIEND, **EVE,** DANCE THROUGH SPACE, YOU CAN TRACK THEIR FLIGHTS SIMPLY BY LISTENING TO THE ROBOTS AND THE SOFT SPURTS OF THE FIRE EXTINGUISHER THAT PROPELS WALL-E.

Movies contain a soundtrack alongside the pictures on the film. But when soundtracks became more layered, it presented a problem. Moviemakers couldn't make movie film wider to handle more audio tracks. The solution? Piggyback. Engineers figured out how to encode four audio channels onto only two tracks. As you'd expect, the left track streams sound to the left speakers, and the right track streams to the right speakers. The sound for the center channel is recorded on both tracks, and a decoder in the speaker system picks out the signal and streams it to the central speakers.

TRACKS

Most films carry both digital and nondigital, or analog, soundtracks so that they can be played by any movie theater's projection system.

The stereo analog soundtrack runs along the left side of the images and just inside the holes on the edge of the film.

The digital soundtrack is coded into strips on the edges of the film.

FUN FACT

● Sound artist Susan Philipsz creates haunting **"audio collages."** The sound artworks, installed in public spaces, are designed to tap into **listeners' emotions,** prompting them to ponder big questions.

How Things Worked

Walt Disney's iconic *Fantasia*, the 1940 animated film set to classical music, pioneered surround sound. To make the film, the sound engineer took separate recordings of each section of the symphony orchestra and mixed them to produce four audio soundtracks. Film back then wasn't able to handle four soundtracks, so Disney recorded the soundtracks on a separate reel of film, which movie cinemas had to play alongside the movie. Each soundtrack played through different speakers positioned around the theater, so musical themes seemed to move from one section of the orchestra to another. Few cinemas could play *Fantasia* because it needed expensive speaker systems—in its early showings, 54 speakers! Disney later scaled back the film's sound to a simpler, seven-channel sound that more theaters could handle. But *Fantasia* showed what was possible and sparked a race to develop surround-sound methods to create a more realistic moviegoing experience.

TRY THIS!

Sound travels on waves, and we can tell a lot about a sound's source by how its waves reach us. Here's a fun experiment to see—or hear—how it works. Get a friend and a three-foot (1-m)-long piece of clean hose that's an inch (2.5 cm) or more across. (Pool or spa hose works really well.) Hold the two ends of the hose over your ears and let the rest of it loop behind your head. Have your friend tap different places on the hose with a pencil. Try to guess when the center of the hose is tapped. How far does your friend have to move off center before you can tell it's closer to one ear? Now try listening with only one ear, and see if you can tell where your friend is tapping.

It's a lot easier to tell where a sound is coming from when we use both ears. That's because it takes the sound waves a tiny bit of time to travel to our ears. If the sound originates closer to, say, your right ear, its sound waves reach your right ear a tiny bit sooner than your left, clueing your brain to the sound's original location.

PROFILE: Dayna Grant

STUNT PERFORMER

Dayna Grant isn't your typical mom. For her, a day might involve getting dragged under a monster truck, thrown off a balcony, or attacked by a gang of angry swordsmen.

She wouldn't have it any other way.

Dayna is an award-winning stuntwoman. She's thrilled audiences for two decades with her work in numerous movies and television shows, including *The Chronicles of Narnia: The Lion, the Witch*

> ## "A DAY MIGHT INVOLVE GETTING DRAGGED UNDER A MONSTER TRUCK..."

and the Wardrobe; Power Rangers; King Kong; and Xena: Warrior Princess.

Not that you'd recognize her.

Dayna steps in when it's too dangerous for an actress to do part of her role—and we're not supposed to notice when that happens. Dayna wears an identical costume as the actress, and the director makes sure not to show her face for too long.

"I'm there ideally to make my actress look as good as possible," she says.

Sometimes that means teaching the actress to fake a punch. But most of the time, it means Dayna takes over the risky parts.

Leaping from a building while on fire? Her all-time favorite stunt. (She wears a fireproof suit.) Flying through the air on a wire? She loves it. She'll gallop through a dark forest on horseback or do back flips during a kung fu fight. Nothing gets to her.

She has the knowledge, skills, and experience to do the stunt work—and to do it safely. It comes from years of training and a deep understanding of how human bodies are built and what they can do.

Sometimes she'll need to learn a new skill, like archery or driving a chariot. But that's part of what makes the work exciting.

"The reason I love stunts is that every day is different," she says. "You never know what you're going to get."

A NATURAL

Dayna grew up on horseback. Before she could walk, she rode. Her dad made her a special saddle that held her securely on the horse's back. Even if she fell asleep, she couldn't fall off!

He didn't only teach her to ride. He also taught her that if you fall off a horse, you get right back on. That lesson—be tough and never give up—helped her become one of the top stunt performers in the world.

Like all stunt performers 20 years ago, Dayna learned

on the job. Unlike now, stunts were rarely rehearsed before filming back then. She got hurt sometimes, but she learned how to get it right.

"Before doing any stunt, I'll visualize it," she says. "A lot of the times we only get one, maybe two shots at it. So we don't want to muck it up."

When she was 18 years old, she auditioned for the TV show *Xena: Warrior Princess*, which was filmed in New Zealand, her home country. She hardly knew anything about stunt work, but she got the job. One success followed another, and she landed bigger roles on television and movies.

The work can be grueling. She may be away from home for six to nine months on a film. But she's managed to bring her family with her—to Hungary, Namibia, and England—so she could spend her days off with her kids.

Dayna remembers one day when her son came home from school and told her, "'I've just realized you're not a normal mum. You jump off buildings and set yourself on fire.' He had thought that was normal."

Normal or not, Dayna wouldn't trade her job for any other. It's tough to break into stunt work, but the reward is worth all the hard knocks on the path to success, she says. "You just get back on the horse again and just keep going."

DAYNA IS PASSING ALONG HER KNOWLEDGE TO THE **NEXT GENERATION** OF STUNT PERFORMERS. SHE RUNS THE NEW ZEALAND **STUNT SCHOOL,** AND SHE COORDINATES STUNTS FOR SOME MOVIES.

A NATIVE NEW ZEALANDER— OR "KIWI"— DAYNA'S HERITAGE IS MAORI, THE **INDIGENOUS** POLYNESIAN PEOPLE OF THE ISLAND NATION.

IN ADDITION TO **HORSEBACK RIDING,** DAYNA DID **GYMNASTICS** WHEN SHE WAS YOUNG. SHE STILL USES THE MOVES IN HER STUNT WORK.

on the set of *The Chronicles of Narnia*

HIGH-TECH PUPPETS

How does ANIMATRONICS create real-looking characters?

Dig In

How'd you like to sing a duet with a robin? Maybe bike through the air with an alien? Or have a *Brachiosaurus* sneeze all over you? (OK, maybe not that last one.) If you're a fan of *Mary Poppins*, *E.T.*, or *Jurassic Park*, you know what we're talking about. They're classic scenes—and they're all thanks to the awesome art and technology of animatronics. Take a look at some of Hollywood's most amazing characters.

Why do movie-makers use animatronics ?

How do you make animatronic characters ?

Do they really work like puppets ?

173

Hybrids

Take puppets and robots and put them together, and you get animatronics. Animatronic characters move like real creatures, interacting with actors on set during filming—a big advantage over computer-generated images. They're used when real creatures don't exist, like extraterrestrials or extinct dinosaurs, or when it would be too dangerous, expensive, or impossible for characters to do something, even if it's as simple as a bird singing a song without flying away.

Robo-Puppet

Animatronics may be operated by puppeteers—sometimes hiding inside them!—or by remote control or computer programs. Some animatronic devices may only do a few things and may be only part of a creature, such as a dinosaur head used for close-up shots. Others are complete, life-size creatures with a full range of movements. Early animatronic characters look pretty fake now. But with today's advanced technology, animatronic characters look and act exactly like live creatures—as long as you don't notice all the puppeteers working their magic.

ANIMATRONIC ALL-STARS

Animatronic creatures star in many blockbuster movies, but they didn't start off in film. The first animatronic characters were attractions at fairs and amusement parks. Check out these milestones in animatronics.

1939: Sparko, the Robot Dog, and a galloping horse (who remained nameless) wow crowds at the 1939 World's Fair in New York. They're the first modern animatronic characters.

1955: Disney, a pioneer in animatronics, uses animatronic animals in the Jungle Cruise ride at Disneyland and, in 1963, features animatronic birds in the Enchanted Tiki Room at the theme park.

1964: The first fully completed animatronic human character, Abraham Lincoln, impresses crowds at the World's Fair in New York. An updated model takes up residence at Disneyland, where it gives five performances each hour.

1964: Animatronics debuts on the big screen in *Mary Poppins*, where the magical nanny sings a duet with an animatronic robin perched on her finger. Controls for the bird run under the actress's sleeves.

1975: An animatronic shark terrorizes the seas in *Jaws*. Problems with the three shark devices—nicknamed "Bruce"—force the movie director to limit the number of shots showing the entire beast, but that only adds to the suspense. The movie becomes a classic thriller.

1993: *Jurassic Park* breaks new ground with life-size animatronic dinosaurs that look amazingly—and terrifyingly—realistic. The movie series continues to push the technology in its sequels.

2007: *Walking with Dinosaurs* brings life-size dinosaurs into arenas around the world. The live show is based on a hit 1999 BBC series, but the TV series actually relied heavily on computer-generated images, mixed with some animatronics, to create its TV dinosaurs.

FUN FACT

THE MASSIVE ANIMATRONIC *SPINOSAURUS* IN 2001's *JURASSIC PARK III* WAS AS **LONG AS A SCHOOL BUS,** MEASURING 43.5 FEET (13.3 M) LONG AND WEIGHING A WHOPPING 24,000 POUNDS (10,886 KG OR 12 TONS)—AS MUCH AS TWO AFRICAN ELEPHANTS.

ARTS AND SCIENCE

Before a puppeteer or computer scientist can bring an animatronic creature to life, teams of artists, engineers, and mechanics must make the mechanized puppet—a process that can take up to a year.

Artists design the creature portrayed in the story. They often use a computer program that makes a 3-D model. To make it realistic, they study animal anatomy and movements.

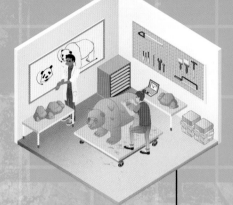

An actual model, based on the computer model, is made of foam. Sculptors shape it and add details, like wrinkles in the skin and creases where it would move.

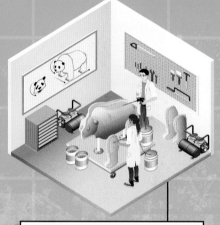

A mold is made by putting fiber-glass cloth onto the sculpture. Once it dries, mold-makers split the mold apart and line the inside to make space for the skin.

Foam rubber is pumped into the mold to create the creature's body. It's put in a big oven over-night to dry it into shape and then the mold is removed.

The insides of the creature are carved out to make room for the mechanical parts that hold it upright and make it move.

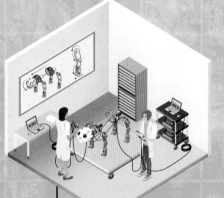

The creature is assembled. Metal parts hold it upright, and mechanical parts are fitted inside the body so it can move. A skin is slipped over the outside.

Artists paint multiple layers on the rubbery skin, first using paint spray guns made for cars, and then air brushes for shading. Details—such as wrinkles, scars, and blem-ishes—are added with ever finer brushes. Artists model skin tones after real animals.

A team of puppeteers work together, usually using remote controls, to make the creature move. Each puppeteer works only one small part.

WANT TO KNOW MORE?

TELL ME MORE

POWERED UP

Animatronic characters are works of engineering genius. An internal frame, often created to mimic a natural skeleton, supports the character and all the internal mechanisms needed to make it move. Various mechanical systems move every part of the animatronic character, and custom-made electronics, connected to the control systems, tell the mechanical systems when to move and how. The character is like a big remote-controlled toy!

TEAMWORK

You don't control a life-size dinosaur by yourself. Complex animatronics, like you see in movies, require a whole team of puppeteers, each one controlling only a part of the creature. They're like a band, in which each musician plays a different part but all the parts come together to make a great song. Some animatronic characters are worn by a puppeteer (or two) like a costume. Animatronic characters that you see in theme parks (or in pizza joints) run on computer programs.

How Things Worked

Animatronic characters are seriously high-tech, but they have roots going back centuries to automata, mechanized devices that looked like animals or people and moved on their own. Ancient Chinese texts written in the fifth and third centuries B.C. mention automata, and the ancient Greeks also made simple automata, like a life-size maid that filled a cup when it was put in her hand. It wasn't until the 13th through 18th centuries that automata performed complex movements. In the 12th century, the Islamic scientist and inventor Al-Jazari built a number of complex automata, including a band of mechanical musicians and an elephant-shaped clock with a little man that struck a bell and a bird that chirped to note the passage of time. Al-Jazari used flowing water to power some machines and controlled their movements by mounting egg-shaped discs on a rotating rod (a camshaft), which moved levers and pistons inside the automata. Not long afterward, Europeans included automata in clocks, like the famous Prague Astronomical Clock, which included biblical figures as well as a skeleton, a figure of death, which struck a bell to mark the time. By the 15th century, automata were all the rage. Leonardo da Vinci built a mechanical knight that could raise its visor and two automata lions: one that reared up on its hind legs and presented lilies to the king of France and another that walked on its own. But perhaps the most amazing automaton was built by Henri Maillardet, a Swiss clockmaker who lived in London. It was a mechanical boy that could draw four different pictures or write three poems. Maillardet used camshafts, like those invented by Al-Jazari, to move the boy's hand.

FUN FACTS

● Walt Disney's **animatronic Abraham Lincoln** fooled people attending the 1964 World's Fair in New York. No, they knew it wasn't the long-dead president, but they did think it was a real person— an actor in costume.

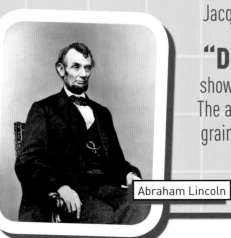

Abraham Lincoln

● In 1739, French inventor Jacques de Vaucanson built a **mechanical "Digesting Duck"** to show how living animals work. The automaton "ate" kernels of grain, which later ... um, came out its other end.

THE GUTS

If you open up an animatronic creature, you won't find slimy organs and blood vessels. (Whew!) You'll see an amazing construction of metal, plastic, and advanced circuitry.

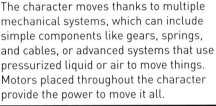

For parts operated by remote control, electronic circuits relay the control instructions from the puppeteers to the motors.

The character moves thanks to multiple mechanical systems, which can include simple components like gears, springs, and cables, or advanced systems that use pressurized liquid or air to move things. Motors placed throughout the character provide the power to move it all.

The frame, which supports the character and all the mechanisms needed to move it, is often made of steel, plastic, or graphite, a strong, lightweight material.

How do you tell the difference between computer-generated imagery (CGI) and animatronics? If you can see **the creature's entire body,** it's probably part CGI. Large animatronics move on tracks or vehicles; you **never see their feet.**

Actor **Johnny Depp,** who plays Captain Jack Sparrow in the *Pirates of the Caribbean* movies, sometimes sneaks into the **ride at Disneyland** and takes the place of the animatronic Captain Jack character.

GOING IN DEPTH

How do movies create 3-D IMAGES on a flat screen?

Dig In

The world isn't flat. (Duh.) So why should movies be confined to a flat screen? Lucky for us, many movie directors think they shouldn't. Advances in 3-D technology put us into the movie's world—and sometimes make movie characters jump into ours. It takes some amazing tech to make it happen, both in the camera and in the theater. Let's take a look. No need to wear funky glasses.

How do movie cameras film in 3-D **?**

Why do we have to wear those weird glasses to watch 3-D movies **?**

Can a regular movie projector show a 3-D movie **?**

JUST THE FACTS

Insightful

You see in three dimensions (3-D) because of a brilliant arrangement between your brain and eyes. Each eye sees the world from a slightly different perspective. Your brain takes those two images and rebuilds them into a 3-D view. It gives you depth perception—or stereopsis—so you can tell, for example, that the little speck you see is actually a Great Dane down the block instead of an ant-size pooch nearby. To shoot a movie in 3-D, movie directors use cameras that act like our eyes. They have two lenses (sometimes two cameras) positioned side by side to capture two images from slightly different angles.

CAMERA EYES

Advanced 3-D movie cameras mimic the way our eyes work to capture a scene in realistic three dimensions.

Two lenses are mounted side by side, about as far apart as our eyes, to "see" the scene like we would. Like our eyes, the lenses turn inward to view things close up or straight ahead for objects in the distance. The lenses capture digital images, coded as electronic signals.

A small computer inside the camera coordinates the lens and camera operations.

The camera, which weighs about 25 to 30 pounds (11 to 14 kg), can be worn by the camera operator or movie director. It also can be mounted on a stand or a "Steadi-cam" rig that camera operators wear to reduce jiggles.

Controls on the hand grips control the camera's zoom and focus.

"4-D" refers to a 3-D movie with added physical effects that you feel in your seat, like splashes of water, wind blowing, or the rumbling of volcanoes. It's a fun experience—but it's not what scientists think of as a true **"FOURTH DIMENSION."**

FUN FACT

IN THE 1800s, A POPULAR FORM OF ENTERTAINMENT WAS LOOKING THROUGH A **STEREOSCOPE**, A DEVICE THAT HELD **TWO PHOTOGRAPHS** SIDE BY SIDE TO CREATE A 3-D IMAGE.

STEALING THE SHOW

A 3-D movie theater is designed to trick your brain into seeing 3-D. The projector shines the two separate images captured by the camera up on the screen at the same time. Older technology uses one projector that flickers back and forth between the two images, but more advanced technology uses two-lens cameras that project both images on the screen at the same time. The 3-D glasses filter the two images so each eye sees only the image meant for it. Then, just like in real life, your brain takes those two separate images and stitches them back into a 3-D view.

SINGLED OUT

3-D projectors show two images on the screen, but the filters in 3-D glasses let each of our eyes see only the image meant for it. Since we see the world this way—each eye seeing a slightly different perspective—our brains create depth perception by combining the two images.

TRY THIS!

We're so used to how our eyes and brain work together to see one 3-D view of the world that it's hard to believe our eyes actually see two separate views. But here's a quick and easy way to get more ... shall we say, perspective ... on the matter. Hold your pointer finger up in front of your face. Hold it pretty close, but not so close that it's uncomfortable or you see double. Hold your finger still and alternate closing one eye then the other. It looks a bit like your finger is moving side to side, but it's really the different viewing perspectives of each eye. The effect is easier to see closer up than far away.

Myth vs. FACT

MYTH: Old-time 3-D films were viewed with red-and-blue glasses.

FACT: Yes, but ... not as much as we all seem to think. You may have seen the photos: A 1950s audience stares through cardboard 3-D glasses at a movie screen. They all look a little freaky because one lens of their glasses is red, and the other is blue (or maybe greenish). Those different color glasses (which have a fancy name: anaglyph) can, indeed, be used to view 3-D images, but only the kind created with two differently colored images. Each lens blocked certain colors so only one image made it to each eye. The thing is that by the 1950s, 3-D movies used a different technology (though the red-and-blue glasses never went away completely). The reason many people associate 3-D with those funky red-and-blue glasses is actually because they were used with popular 3-D comic books back in the 1950s (and still with some today) and some 3-D TV in more recent years. The real mystery is why so many people swear they saw photos of 1950s movie audiences wearing them. Photographs from that era were black-and-white.

CHARACTER CREATION

How does ANIMATION tell stories?

Dig In

Animation brings us some of the most amazing movies. Oh, yes, you've got your beasts and lion kings, fair maidens who hang out with dwarf miners, and snow queens who chill with icy spells—and don't forget those toys that come alive when you're not looking. (We always suspected.) They're all awesome in their own right. But they're just the beginning. Animation also brings us a whole zoo of mythical and magical characters in live-action movies, too. Let's find out how.

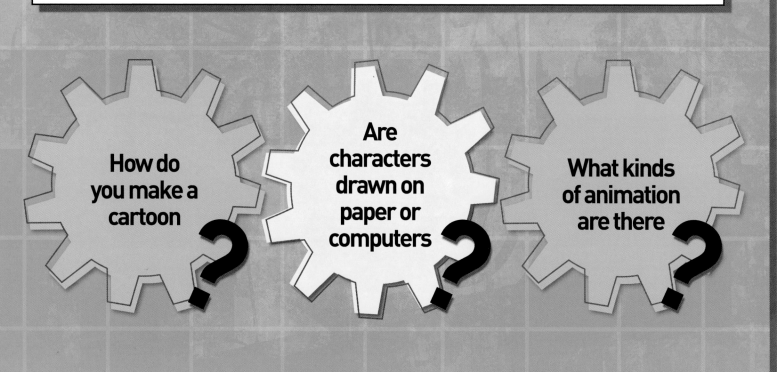

How do you make a cartoon **?**

Are characters drawn on paper or computers **?**

What kinds of animation are there **?**

Storytelling

A cartoon may only last a few minutes, but it takes months to create it—and full-length animated features take years! Both start with a story, of course. Artists first sketch out the story's scenes on a storyboard, a kind of visual outline of the story. They use those sketches to create an "animatic," an early version of the cartoon or film that includes the scenes, maybe a soundtrack, but no developed animation. If they like what they see, they polish the art and add the animation and full soundtrack, which includes dialogue recorded by actors, special effects, and music.

What a Character!

While artists work on the story, animators develop the characters. They often work off sketches that an art director drew based on descriptions in the story, but they usually create the characters on computers using specialized programs that help them add the characters' movements. Animators work on many details to make the character look real: facial features, the texture of its clothes, shadows, you name it. It takes months just to get the character's mouth to move along with the actor's dialogue.

ANIMATION FOR ALL

Animation is **almost as varied** as the stories it helps to tell. Here are some popular forms:

Traditional cell animation:
Artists hand-draw every frame, changing the art slightly with each frame to create a sequence, much like the drawings in a flip book. Characters often are traced to create fluid movement. It's how classic cartoons and animated features were created.

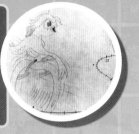

2-D animation:
It's simple animation based on combinations of lines and shapes and created in computer programs. Popular for web cartoons, the animation can be created frame by frame or with a rig (a character's computerized skeleton), which makes it easy to move one part, like a leg, at a time.

3-D or computer animation:
The most common type of animation today, it requires animators to have technical computer skills. The animator creates a character in a computer program and moves it, much like a digital puppet, from key position to key position, allowing the computer to add in-between frames.

Stop motion:
Similar to traditional cell animation, it tells a story frame by frame but uses real objects instead of drawings. Animators pose the object, take a picture of it, move it a little and take another picture. Stop motion uses clay characters (claymation), paper cutouts, puppets, toy figures, or even posed people.

FUN FACT

OLD **BLACK-AND-WHITE MOVIES** SOMETIMES USED STOP-MOTION ANIMATION FOR SCENES THAT REQUIRED **"MAGIC."**

PERFECT PLANNING

Making a storyboard—a type of graphic organizer—is an important step in planning a cartoon or movie. It helps the director and artists visualize the key scenes. Storyboards can be drawn or created digitally on a computer.

The Adventures of Super Kitten

Dialogue/
"That cat is a hero!"
"You saved my life!"
"How can I ever repay you??"

Action/
- cameras flash
- super kitten poses
Super Kitten takes off!

Timing/
Whoosh! → 2ᵒᵒ

Sound FX/
Flash!
Snap!

Scenes are sketched out in order on the storyboard, much like a comic, so the cartoon or movie director can see how the story will develop visually. It's at this stage that the director may decide to change a scene, like seeing it from a different angle.

Comments and maybe key bits of dialogue are written down under the scenes to help the film's creators see how the story will progress and decide how long a scene should last.

POPEYE, the Sailor Man—the squinting, muscular cartoon hero of comics, cartoons, and a live-action movie—was the first character from newspaper comics to have a statue **ERECTED IN HIS HONOR.** In fact, there are at least five Popeye statues in the U.S.: in Illinois, Texas, and three towns in Arkansas. All the towns are landlocked, so not big into sailing. They must love spinach as much as Popeye does.

FUN FACT

THE ANIMATOR WHO CREATED **BEAST** IN THE ANIMATED FEATURE *BEAUTY AND THE BEAST* USED A LION'S MANE, A **BUFFALO'S BEARD** AND HEAD SHAPE, A WILD BOAR'S TUSKS, A **GORILLA'S BROW,** A BEAR'S BODY, AND A **WOLF'S LEGS** AND **TAIL.**

WANT TO KNOW MORE?

TELL ME MORE

GETTING IN CHARACTER

Animating a character on a computer takes creativity and technical expertise. Animators first create the characters' most important poses—the key frames—the ones that would give you an idea of what's happening in the story even if you didn't see the whole thing. Once the animators are happy with the key frames, they start breaking down the movements from one key frame to the next and add in-between poses. They add as many as it takes to make the movement look good, and then they have the computer program connect the movement between the poses. The animators finish up by smoothing the movements and adding the human touches that bring the characters to life.

How Things Worked

If you've ever created a flip book—in which you draw a sequence of pictures that seem to move when you flip through them—you know the basics about animation. Long before computers were involved, animators created cartoons and full-length animated movies by hand-drawing and coloring thousands of individual pictures. The pictures were photographed one-by-one to create the cartoon or movie, with usually 24 frames flashing by every second of the film. To create smooth movement, the artists had to make sure that the pictures lined up perfectly, with the characters moving only slightly from frame to frame. To pull that off, they traced a new frame from the one that came before it, making tiny changes to show movement. Artists worked on a glass table lighted from below and traced in pencil on thin paper. After they finished the detailed line drawings (and the movie director approved them), the drawings were copied in ink on a clear plastic film, originally made of celluloid—which gave this technique its name: cel animation. The cels were flipped over and painted. When it came time to photograph the pictures for the film, the cels were laid on painted backgrounds. This cel-animation technique traces its roots to the first modern animation in 1914, a cartoon called *Gertie the Dinosaur*. Cartoonist Winsor McCay drew more than 10,000 frames to bring the cantanKerous dino to life, but it was worth the effort. His work inspired future animators, including Walt Disney. Disney pushed the development of cel animation, especially with his 1928 cartoon *Steamboat Willie*, which starred Mickey Mouse, and then in 1937 with the first full-length animated feature, *Snow White and the Seven Dwarfs*. It took a team of 32 lead animators—and hundreds of other artists working on in-between frames, cel inking and painting, backgrounds, and more—to create the more than 250,000 paintings used to bring the fairy tale to the big screen.

SKIN AND BONES

Animators don't only draw the outside of characters, they put skeletons inside them, too. They're not being crazy. The skeletons help them animate the characters on the computer. They don't show up in the final cartoon or film—unless, of course, the character is an actual skeleton!

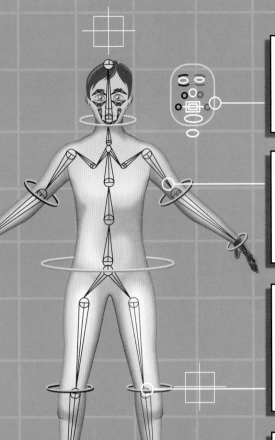

Many parts of the skeleton, or rig, match up with where bones would be in a real person or animal. But additional rigging is added to make fine movements, like FACIAL FEATURES.

The skeleton, also known as a RIG, is similar to a stick figure that the animator can move like a marionette puppet—only instead of strings, it has digital lines and dots connected to the computer program.

Each part of the skeleton has a POINT, called an animation variable or "avar," which the animator positions for each key frame. The computer animation software program uses those points to help fill in the movement between key frames.

The character's SURFACE, also called its skin or mesh, is where the artistry comes in. The animator adds colors, textures, shadows, and other details—even a sparkle in the character's eye.

FUN FACTS

The computer-animated character **Woody in *Toy Story*** had 700 skeleton points, or animation variables (avars). To create Woody's facial expression, animators used **100 avars** in his face alone!

Back in the mid-1800s, people oohed and aahed at an **early form** of animation called the **zoetrope,** a spinning cylinder with a series of pictures or photographs inside that produced the **illusion of motion.**

TALES FROM THE LAB

ACTING PLUS ANIMATION

BRINGING CREATURES TO LIFE

Movies transport us to worlds where fire-breathing dragons hoard gold, house elves protect wizards, and big, friendly giants roam the night.

Moviemakers need those creatures to be real to us. But ... how? They can't ask the casting office to send them a trained dragon!

In today's movies, that process takes a lot of high-tech computer wizardry. But the idea of combining a real actor's movements with animation is actually a century old.

THE HUMAN TOUCH

In the early 1900s, animation pioneer Max Fleischer watched cartoons in movie theaters and thought the characters' movements were too stiff and jerky. He knew he could do better.

> ## "THEY CAN'T ASK THE CASTING OFFICE TO SEND THEM A TRAINED DRAGON!"

He filmed his brother Dave acting out a funny scene in a clown suit. Then Max projected each frame of the live-action film onto an easel and traced Dave's motions, using them to give his cartoon clown more realistic movements.

His short cartoons were amazing, and they grabbed the attention of another animator, Walt Disney. In 1937, Walt Disney Productions used Max's technique, called rotoscoping, to make Snow White swirl and twirl, dancing with her diminutive friends. The full-length, animated *Snow White and the Seven Dwarfs* was groundbreaking. And a big hit.

COMPUTER POWER

In 1997, the animated film *Sinbad: Beyond the Veil of Mists* changed moviemaking forever. It pioneered a motion-capture technique that uses computers instead of tracing by hand.

Actors wear skin-tight suits covered in tracking markers. Multiple cameras record them, and computers generate 3-D "skeletons" that move like the markers did. Animators draw digital characters on the skeletons. It lets actors play any character—no matter the size, shape, or even species. Ninja turtles? Two-story-tall mountain gorillas? No problem.

In 1999, this technique put Jar-Jar Binks, the first fully digital main character in a live-action movie, in *Star Wars Episode 1: The Phantom Menace*. Ahmed Best, who portrayed Jar-Jar, actually acted alone in a movie studio, and Jar-Jar was digitally inserted into the movie.

MAKING IT REAL

Actors are great at playing make-believe, of course, but it's easier if they can interact on the set.

So actor Andy Serkis, who played Gollum for 2002's *The Lord of the Rings: The Two Towers* (another milestone), acted with the other actors, who wore wizard, hobbit, elf, and dwarf costumes. Then Andy played his part again in a studio for motion capture. Still, animators had to create Gollum's squints and snarls by hand, frame by frame, from Andy's filmed performance.

To capture the emotions revealed by glares, flaring nostrils, tight lips, and so on, moviemakers put motion-capture markers on actors' faces. But digital artists always had to improve upon the computer-generated images.

In 2009, *Avatar* broke new ground. Actors wore lightweight helmets that held small cameras in front of their faces. The technology transferred the actors' expressions to their Na'vi characters. Animators only needed to add ears and tails.

Three years later, in 2012, actor Andy Serkis again portrayed Gollum for *The Hobbit: An Unexpected Journey*. Dressed in a motion-capture suit and a camera-helmet, Andy played Gollum on the set with the other actors. Technology captured his every creep, grimace, and wince. *Motion* capture had become true *performance* capture.

NEVER HEARD OF THE **GROUNDBREAKING** *SINBAD: BEYOND THE VEIL OF MISTS?* YOU'RE NOT ALONE. **IT WAS A FLOP** AT THE BOX OFFICE.

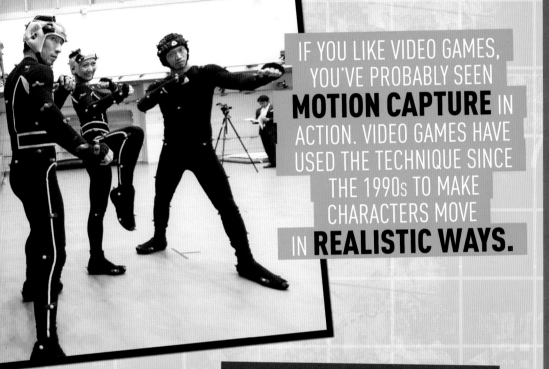

IF YOU LIKE VIDEO GAMES, YOU'VE PROBABLY SEEN **MOTION CAPTURE** IN ACTION. VIDEO GAMES HAVE USED THE TECHNIQUE SINCE THE 1990s TO MAKE CHARACTERS MOVE IN **REALISTIC WAYS.**

Make It BETTER!

Moviemakers who use computer-generated characters face a challenge. If a character looks a lot like a human but something is a little off (maybe the eyes look dull, the skin too slick, or the mouths empty), it seriously creeps us out. And not in a good way. It's a problem known in Hollywood—and robotics—as the "uncanny valley." We're fine if the character is a cartoon or strange creature. But when something's wrong with a human-looking character, we can't relate to it.

The challenge for moviemakers is to get us to believe the character is a real, emotional being. Capturing an actor's facial performance helps moviemakers create more realistic-looking characters. What else do you think they can they do to make a convincing character? If you were a moviemaker, what would you change about computer-generated characters?

ACTOR BENEDICT CUMBERBATCH STUDIED REPTILES AT THE **LONDON ZOO** BEFORE HE PLAYED THE GOLD-HOARDING DRAGON **SMAUG** IN *THE HOBBIT: THE DESOLATION OF SMAUG.*

TO DEVELOP THE **CREEPY VOICE** OF GOLLUM, ACTOR ANDY SERKIS WAS **INSPIRED** BY THE SOUND **HIS CAT** MADE WHEN COUGHING UP A FUR BALL.

COMPUTER SCIENTISTS ARE **IMPROVING** PERFORMANCE CAPTURE TECHNOLOGIES THAT **DON'T REQUIRE** ACTORS TO WEAR MOTION-CAPTURE SUITS OR TRACKING MARKERS ALL OVER **THEIR FACES.**

LISTEN UP!

How do **FOLEY SOUNDS** add to a movie's effects?

Dig In

Imagine this movie scene: A pirate ship bounds over stormy seas, waves crashing against its bow, its sails flapping in the wind. It overtakes an unlucky galleon, and the pirates swing over on rope lines, where they engage the crew in an epic sword battle. You don't just see this action, you hear it: waves crashing, swords clashing. Those sounds aren't recorded on the ship. They're made by Foley artists working in a sound studio. Let's listen in.

Why don't movie-makers record the actual sounds?

How do Foley artists make the different sounds?

When are the sounds recorded?

JUST THE FACTS

Sound Logic

Why don't moviemakers just record real sounds: the zing of swords as actors battle, a crack of thunder, the roar of a *Tyrannosaurus rex*? Um, wait a minute, there's a problem: No *T. rex* to record. How about those swords? Probably rubber props. Definitely not clangy or zingy. And standing outside during a thunderstorm holding a microphone up in the air? Not advised! Foley artists reproduce those sounds to add to a movie's soundtrack. On set, sound technicians focus on capturing the actors' dialogue, even if they're whispering. They place microphones to pick up the actors—not background noises.

Faking It

Foley artists supply the sounds that make movies sound real. The sounds are realistic, but they're not real. That horse galloping across the screen? A Foley artist produced the hoof beats by clomping wood blocks or coconut shells together. Foley artists use everyday materials—even their own voices—to reproduce all sorts of sounds. They often watch a movie in a sound studio and create the sounds as the action occurs on the big screen.

Foley artists create the sound of galloping horses for a radio program, 1940.

The movie *WALL-E* may be set far in the **FUTURE,** but the sound effects weren't made with space-age technology. An **OLD ARMY RADIO GENERATOR** created the sound of the **LITTLE ROBOT** moving slowly, while a biplane starter motor produced the sound of his faster movements.

FUN FACT

FOLEY SOUNDS ARE NAMED AFTER **JACK FOLEY,** A FORMER RADIO SOUND EFFECTS ARTIST WHO BECAME A PIONEER IN PRODUCING SOUND EFFECTS WHEN MOVIEMAKERS SWITCHED FROM MAKING SILENT MOVIES TO "**TALKIES**" IN THE 1920s.

STUDIO MAGIC

It's up to Foley artists and sound engineers to create almost all the sounds for a movie or television show. On set, sound technicians place microphones to capture the actors' dialogue. The other sound effects are left for studio work.

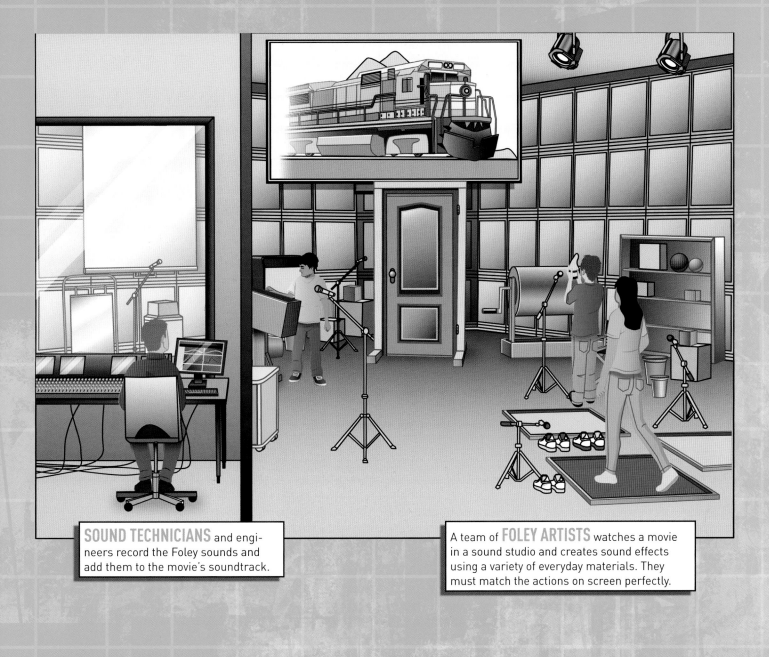

SOUND TECHNICIANS and engineers record the Foley sounds and add them to the movie's soundtrack.

A team of FOLEY ARTISTS watches a movie in a sound studio and creates sound effects using a variety of everyday materials. They must match the actions on screen perfectly.

FUN FACT

THE FIRST SOUND ARTISTS **CREATED SOUND EFFECTS** FOR DRAMAS BROADCAST **LIVE ON RADIO** IN THE 1920s. BACK THEN, NO TECHNOLOGY EXISTED FOR RECORDING THE SOUND EFFECTS IN ADVANCE, SO THE ARTISTS CREATED THEM LIVE.

WANT TO KNOW MORE?

NOISEMAKERS

Foley artists work in a special studio so that only the sounds they create end up on the recording. (They wouldn't want the sounds of a passing car or office phone making it into the movie's soundtrack!) The Foley track is only one part of the movie's soundtrack, which also includes specially created sound effects, intentional background noise, music and, of course, the actors' dialogue. To feel natural, the Foley effects must match the movements on the screen. Foley artists may use real props for some sounds, for example, "walking" hard-soled shoes across a table for footsteps. But they often use everyday materials in new ways. Rattling a large steel sheet creates the sound of thunder, crinkling cellophane sounds like a crackling fire, scraping a large nail across a sheet of glass screeches like brakes. Sometimes Foley artists create simple sound props, like a box full of broken junk that makes a great crashing sound when dropped, or machines that create special sounds, like blowing wind.

The REAL DEAL

Foley sounds are sound effects, but not all sound effects are Foley sounds. Yes, some people use the term "Foley" for everything. But that's not quite accurate. Some sound effects, or "FX," are noises that sound engineers add by themselves to a movie's soundtrack. They make the sound effects on a computer or take them from a digital library of prerecorded sounds. The sound engineer adds them to the movie where needed, adjusting their volume and length to fit. It's possible for a sound engineer to mix in almost all the sound effects—but it's not necessarily a good idea. It's quicker to rely on Foley artists, who often can provide the sounds in real time as they watch a movie. In general, Foley artists make most of the sounds associated with people or animals—footsteps, rustling clothes, sword fights, and even people kissing—while sound engineers add in the space-age sounds and big blasts. But the line between Foley sounds and sound FX is blurry. Who does what depends on the sound studio and the particular movie being shot. Take the example of a horse whinnying. Some Foley artists whinny as well as an equine, but sometimes moviemakers will record an actual horse instead. Still other movies insert a prerecorded whinny from a digital library. As for those unnatural sounds, Foley artists still may be involved. They sometimes help create an unusual sound by performing complex sound sequences that would take sound engineers a long time to mix alone, and sometimes engineers distort Foley sounds for a special effect.

TRY THIS!

Foley artists often use everyday things to create sound effects—and so can you! Watch a favorite movie or cartoon with the volume turned off and supply your own sound effects. It's easy—and a lot of fun to do with friends or family members. Here are some Foley artist tricks of the trade to get you started: Put hard-soled shoes on your hands and walk them on a table to create footsteps, flap a pair of rubber gloves to sound like birds flying, rattle a metal cookie sheet for thunder, stir a bucket of water to create ocean sounds, whack garden trowels together for swords, or rub two sheets of sandpaper together to sound like a train. Experiment! What other sounds can you create?

STORMY

Foley artists create many sounds using everyday materials, but they've also built devices to produce sounds that are harder to create. Most of the unusual sounds today are pulled from digital libraries of sound effects, but Foley artists got pretty creative in the past. Check out how they made some storm effects.

WIND
A cylinder made of wood slats spaced out and covered with silk created a whirring wind sound when a Foley artist cranked a handle on the side.

RAIN
A long box filled with pebbles—much like a rain stick—was tilted back and forth to make the pebbles tumble to the far end, creating a sound like rain.

THUNDER
A large, thin sheet of metal could be rattled, producing the loud rumble of thunder.

FUN FACTS

● **Sound designer** Ben Burtt, who worked on *Star Wars*, accidentally discovered the perfect humming sound for the **light sabers.** He moved a microphone **too close** to a TV picture tube, and it created sound interference. He mixed that weird noise with the sound of a **projector** to get the light saber.

● The **high-tech** sound of doors sliding open on *Star Trek*'s Enterprise spaceship was created by pulling a **sheet of paper** out of an envelope.

TRY THIS!

DIRECTOR FOR A DAY

CREATE YOUR OWN STOP-MOTION ANIMATED MOVIE

Stop motion is a special type of animation. It uses real objects—instead of drawings or computer-generated images—to tell a story. The story characters can be people, animals, or even everyday objects. You can make them out of clay or paper or just use some toy figures, puppets, or even friends whom you pose. Give it a try, and be creative! That's what movie-making is all about.

Want to see this film in action? **Check out:**
natgeokids.com/HowThingsWork

WHAT TO DO

1. GET CREATIVE and brainstorm a short story. Make sure it has a beginning, middle, and end.

2. WRITE DOWN YOUR STORY (or pick one you've already written). If you want to get professional, make a storyboard—rough sketches of the story's key scenes.

3. GATHER OR MAKE THE characters and props you'll need for your movie.

4. PICK A LOCATION WHERE you're going to shoot the movie. Make sure you'll have enough room to take pictures from different angles.

5. FIND OR CREATE ANY backdrops you may want. (Sometimes even a blanket will suffice.)

6. ASK YOUR PARENTS if you can use a stop-motion smartphone app. Seriously recommended: They make the shoot easier and even let you add sound effects. (There are lots of options, but most cost a few dollars.) You can also make a stop-motion movie using a video recorder on a phone or camera. But it's harder, and you'll need to shoot a silent story that moves slowly. If neither of those are options, maybe you could even experiment with creating an awesome flip book by taking still images and printing them.

7. SET UP YOUR FIRST shot. Position your characters and props for your first scene. Put your "movie camera" (what we're calling your smartphone or camera now) on a tripod, if you have one, or figure out a way to keep it steady and in the same place. (Tip: Keep your camera on the same level as the action. Don't shoot the scene from above, unless you're doing a special aerial shot.)

8. WHETHER YOU'RE USING A moviemaking app or not, the process is the same: Take a picture, move your characters a tiny bit to show some action—whatever the story needs—and repeat. If you're using an app, follow its instructions about recording each frame.

9. REPEAT STEP 8 over and over and over until you complete your story. (Tip: If you mess up a shot, no worries. You can just redo that one.)

10. GATHER FAMILY AND FRIENDS and debut your film!

WHAT TO EXPECT

AN ACADEMY AWARD? WELL, MAYBE NOT. BUT YOU'LL HAVE CREATED A WORK OF ART. BUT BEWARE—IT CAN TAKE A LONG TIME TO SHOOT YOUR FILM! ONE TWO-MINUTE VIDEO COULD TAKE AS MUCH AS AN HOUR TO SHOOT.

WHAT'S GOING ON?

WHEN THE INDIVIDUAL PICTURES ARE PLAYED BACK ONE AFTER ANOTHER, THEY CREATE AN ILLUSION THAT YOUR CHARACTERS ARE ACTUALLY MOVING. IF THE PICTURES ARE PLAYED BACK QUICKLY ENOUGH—FOR EXAMPLE, IF YOU USED A STOP-MOTION APP—YOUR BRAIN WILL BLEND THEM TOGETHER, PERCEIVING FAIRLY SMOOTH MOTION.

GLOSSARY

3-D—something that has height, width, and depth—or appears to. (Objects in the real world are three-dimensional, but a drawing or photograph is two-dimensional.)

air pressure—the force exerted on something by the weight of the air

algae—simple, often small plants that grow in or near water and lack true stems, roots, and leaves

antioxidant—a substance that reduces damage caused by chemical reactions involving oxygen

artifact—a culturally or historically interesting object made by a person

atmosphere—the blanket of gases surrounding a planet

atom—the smallest unit of something; the basic building block of matter

bacteria—microscopic living organisms that can be found everywhere

biofluorescence—a glowing light given out by an organism after it absorbs other light, even if it's a different color

bioluminescence—a glowing light created by a chemical reaction inside an organism

buoyancy—an object's ability to float

causeway—a raised path across wet ground

compound machine—a machine that includes multiple simple machines

centrifugal force—the force that pushes something moving on a circular path to the outside, away from the center of its path

density—the amount of mass that is in a certain amount of an object

electron—a very small particle of matter that has a negative electrical charge. It travels around the nucleus (center part) of an atom.

evaporation—when a liquid changes to a gas

extraterrestrial—something from outside Earth or its atmosphere

extremophile—a microorganism adapted to living in conditions of extreme temperatures, such as ice or hot springs, or where chemicals or minerals are highly concentrated, such as salty environments

fermentation—a natural chemical process that occurs when microorganisms break down organic compounds, such as sugar, and convert them into simpler substances

fulcrum—the support on which a lever turns

genetics—the science or study of genes and heredity

geology—the branch of science that studies the Earth—including rocks, layers of soil, and so on—to learn about its history and life

gravity—the force that attracts two objects together, such as the attraction between Earth and an object on or near Earth

kinetic energy—the energy of motion

mesocyclone—a spinning updraft of air inside a thunderstorm that often produces a tornado

microbe—a microorganism—an extremely small living thing that can only be seen using a microscope—especially bacteria

microgravity—when the force of gravity is so weak it results in weightlessness

molecule—the smallest unit of a substance that has all the properties of that substance. A molecule is made of atoms bonded together.

mythology—a collection of myths or traditional stories, such as those dealing with legendary heroes or gods, belonging to a particular culture

orienteering—a recreational activity where you use a compass and map to race to various checkpoints over unknown territory

photon—a tiny particle of light energy

photosynthesis—the process by which green plants convert sunlight, water, and carbon dioxide into the energy they need to grow

potential energy—stored-up energy

reservoir—a large body of contained water that is used as a source of water

simple machine—a basic device that applies force and makes it stronger. The simple machines are the lever, wheel and axle, pulley, inclined plane, wedge, and screw.

sling—a strap used in the shape of a loop to support or lift a weight or to hurl stones or other weapons

sublimation—when a solid changes directly into a gas without going through a liquid stage

superheat—to heat a liquid under pressure above its boiling point without it evaporating

tectonic plates—massive, irregularly shaped slabs of Earth's crust that float and move, sometimes bumping into others and creating mountains, volcanoes, ocean trenches, and earthquakes

vacuum—an empty space from which all the air and other gases have been removed

vapor—the gas state of something that is usually a solid or liquid at room temperature

wind resistance—a type of friction, also known as drag, where air exerts a force against something that's moving

SELECT BIBLIOGRAPHY

These references provide a more in-depth or historical look at some of the topics in this book. They represent a fraction of the sources consulted in researching the book. Most of these sources are intended for adults but are still appropriate for many advanced readers. However, adults should be aware that websites may include advertisements or links to other content.

American Chemical Society. "More flavorful, healthful chocolate could be on its way." EurekAlert!, March 24, 2015, Available online at www.eurekalert.org/pub_releases/2015-03/acs-mfh021915.php.

"Ancient Computer." NOVA HD, Sept. 23, 2014. Available online at www.youtube.com/watch?v=O5_29GTY-ls.

"A New Home on Mars: NASA Langley's Icy Concept for Living on the Red Planet." NASA, Dec. 29, 2016. Available online at www.nasa.gov/feature/langley/a-new-home-on-mars-nasa-langley-s-icy-concept-for-living-on-the-red-planet.

"The Animation Process from 1938." Available online at www.youtube.com/watch?v=M2ORkIrHUbg.

"Antikythera Mechanism." Nature Video (2 parts), Dec. 11, 2008. Available online at www.youtube.com/watch?v=znM0-arQvHc.

Bearne, Suzanne. "It's a good day as a stuntwoman when you don't leave in an ambulance." The Guardian, Sept. 5, 2016. Available online at www.theguardian.com/careers/2016/sep/05/its-a-good- day-as-a-stuntwoman-when-you-dont-leave-in-an-ambulance.

Bennett, Jay. "Almost Everything We Need to Live on Mars Is Already There." Popular Mechanics (June 14, 2016). Available online at www.popularmechanics.com/space/moon-mars/a21330/nasa-wants-martian-resources-for-martian-colony.

Bonné, Jon. "Floyd Zaiger: a fruit innovator to the world." San Francisco Chronicle, June 12, 2011. Available online at www.sfgate.com/bayarea/article/Floyd-Zaiger-a-fruit-innovator-to-the-world-2368432.php.

Burbank, Luther. "Accomplishing the impossible—the plumcot." In Luther Burbank: His Methods and Discoveries and Their Practical Application, 12 vols., 1914. Available online at www.lutherburbankonline.com/V5-C9.html.

Chaikin, Andrew. "The Story of NASA's Jet-Propulsion Backpack." Smithsonian magazine (April 2014). Available online at www.smithsonianmag.com/science-nature/story-nasas-jet-propulsion-backpack-180950190.

Chanute, Octave. "Aerial Navigation." Lecture, Cornell University, May 2, 1890. Available online at todayinsci.com/G/Giffard_Henri/GiffardHenri-Airship-Chanute.htm.

Clark, Kristen. "A Gyroscope Jetpack for Astronauts." IEEE Spectrum, Nov. 23, 2015. Available online at spectrum.ieee.org/video/aerospace/space-flight/a-gyroscope-jetpack-for-astronauts.

Conover, Emily. "The secret behind the sound: Why popcorn 'pops'." Science magazine (Feb. 10, 2015). Available online at www.sciencemag.org/news/2015/02/secret-behind-sound-why-popcorn-pops.

"Creating Gollum." Nature video, Dec. 11, 2013. Available online at www.youtube.com/watch?v=w_Z7YUyCEGE.

"David Gruber." Explorers Biography. National Geographic. Available online at www.nationalgeographic.org/find-explorers/explorers/8D4D39F2/david-gruber.

De Anda, Guillermo. "Caves of the Maya Dead." National Geographic Explorers Symposium, 2012. Available online at video.nationalgeographic.com/video/deanda-maya-lecture-nglive.

Farrell, Scott. "Arms and Men: The Trebuchet." HistoryNet.com, Sept. 5, 2006. Available online at www.historynet.com/weaponry-the-trebuchet.htm.

Fincher, Lew, and Bill Read. "The 1943 'Surprise' Hurricane." NOAA History. Available online at www.history.noaa.gov/stories_tales/surprise.html.

Graf, Mike. Storm: The Awesome Power of Weather. American Education Publishing, 2011.

Granath, Bob. "Hard work, focus helps Rahmani reach for the stars." NASA Kennedy, April 2, 2014. Available online at www.nasa.gov/content/hard-work-focus-helps-rahmani-reach-for-the-stars.

Grant, Dayna. "I'm a Professional Stuntwoman." Video biography. Available online at www.daynastunts.com/bio.

Green, Hank. "Why Are There Bacteria in My Yogurt?" SciShow, May 31, 2016. Available online at www.youtube.com/watch?v=Xs2xGeu6fHc.

Gruber, David. "Glow-in-the-dark sharks and other stunning sea creatures." TED talk, October 2015. Available online at www.ted.com/talks/david_gruber_glow_in_the_dark_sharks_and_other_stunning_sea_creatures/transcript?language=en#t-835457.

Gruber, David. "Scientist at Work: Notes From the Field." New York Times, blog, June-July 2012. Available online at scientistatwork.blogs.nytimes.com/author/david-gruber/?_r=0.

"Guillermo de Anda." Explorers Biography. National Geographic. Available online at www.nationalgeographic.org/find-explorers/explorers/FCE2C515/guillermo-de-anda.

Hammack, Bill. "How a Film Projector Works." Engineer Guy, July 7, 2015. Available online at www.youtube.com/watch?v=En__V0oEJsU.

Harris, Tom. "How Surround Sound Works." How Stuff Works. Available online at electronics.howstuffworks.com/surround-sound1.htm.

Inglis-Arkell, Esther. "The physics of astronaut ice cream." Gizmodo, July 12, 2012. Available online at io9.gizmodo.com/5925360/the-physics-of-astronaut-ice-cream.

"Jules Henri Giffard's Steam Airship." The History Forum. Available online at www.thehistoryforum.com/airships/henri_giffard.

Kaplan, Sarah. "The rocks on Mars suggest it used to look like Earth. What happened?" Washington Post, July 1, 2016. Available online at www.washingtonpost.com/news/speaking-of-science/wp/2016/07/01/the-rocks-on-mars-suggest-it-used-to-look-like-earth-what-happened.

Kaufman, Marc. "How to Give Mars an Atmosphere, Maybe." NASA: Astrobiology at NASA, Life in the Universe, March 9, 2017. Available online at astrobiology.nasa.gov/news/how-to-give-mars-an-atmosphere-maybe.

Lafrance, Adrienne. "The Most Mysterious Object in the History of Technology." The Atlantic (June 20, 2016). Available online at www.theatlantic.com/technology/archive/2016/06/antikythera-mechanism-whoa/487832.

Lallanilla, Marc. "Mystery of Death Valley's 'Sailing Stones' Solved." LiveScience, June 17, 2013. Available online at www.livescience.com/37492-sailing-stones-death-valley-moving-rocks.html.

Letteri, Joe. "Computer animation: Digital heroes and computer-generated worlds." Nature (Dec. 12, 2013). Available online at www.nature.com/nature/journal/v504/n7479/full/504214a.html.

"The Lycurgus Cup." The British Museum. Available online at britishmuseum.tumblr.com/post/120689869617/the-lycurgus-cup.

Macdonald, Fiona. "NASA's Released a Prototype of the Spacesuit Astronauts Will Wear on Mars." Science Alert, Nov. 12, 2015. Available online at www.sciencealert.com/nasa-s-released-a-prototype-of-the-space-suit-astronauts-will-wear-on-mars.

Marchant, Jo. "Decoding the Antikythera Mechanism, the First Computer." Smithsonian (Feb. 2015). Available online at www.smithsonianmag.com/history/decoding-antikythera-mechanism-first-computer-180953979.

Merali, Zeeya. "This 1,600-Year-Old Goblet Shows That the Romans Were Nanotechnology Pioneers." Smithsonian (Sept. 2013). Available online at www.smithsonianmag.com/history/this-1600-year-old-goblet-shows-that-the-romans-were-nanotechnology-pioneers-787224.

Morrison, Geoffrey. "Why lasers are the future (of projectors)." CNET, June 30, 2015. Available online at www.cnet.com/news/why-lasers-are-the-future-of-projectors.

Netburn, Deborah. "The physics of popcorn." Los Angeles Times, Feb. 11, 2015. Available online at www.latimes.com/science/sciencenow/la-sci-sn-popcorn-science-20150210-story.html.

Petranek, Stephen. "Your kids might live on Mars. Here's how they'll survive." TED 2015, March 2015. Available online at www.ted.com/talks/stephen_petranek_your_kids_might_live_on_mars_here_s_how_they_ll_survive.

Pham. Caroline. "Ancient Riddles of the Deep." Flaunt. Available online at itscarolinepham.com/Guillermo-de-Anda.

Price, Derek J. de Solla. "An Ancient Greek Computer." Scientific American (June 1959), pp. 60–67.

The Printing Press." The History Guide: Lectures on Modern European Intellectual History. Available online at www.historyguide.org/intellect/press.html

"R2: Robonaut." NASA. Available online at robonaut.jsc.nasa.gov/R2.

Rahmani, Hibah. Women@NASA profile, NASA.gov. Available at women.nasa.gov/hibah-rahmani.

Ransford, Matt. "The Search for Extraterrestrial Life: a Brief History." Popular Science (June 17, 2008). Available online at www.popsci.com/military-aviation-space/article/2008-06-et-phone-earth.

Sahagun, Louis. "Mystery of how rocks move across Death Valley lake bed solved." Los Angeles Times, Aug. 27, 2014. Available online at www.latimes.com/local/lanow/la-me-ln-rocks-move-death-valley-lake-bed-20140827-story.html.

Salat, Todd. "How the Aurora Borealis Form." Aurora Hunter. Available online at www.aurorahunter.com/how-the-aurora-borealis-form.html.

Samson, Alyssa. "Underwater Archaeologist: Dr. Guillermo de Anda." National Geographic, July 10, 2012. Available online at www.nationalgeographic.org/news/real-world-geography-guillermo-de-anda.

"Science: Love Grilled Cheese or Mac & Cheese? Learn Why Young Cheese Melts Better Than Aged Cheese." America's Test Kitchen, July 30, 2013. Available online at www.youtube.com/watch?v=uAk8InX-R2A.

Sharp, Tim. "The First Powered Airship." Space.com, July 17, 2012. Available online at www.space.com/16623-first-powered-airship.html.

Shields, Aomawa. "How we'll find life on other planets." TED2015, March 2015. Available online at www.ted.com/talks/aomawa_shields_how_we_ll_find_life_on_other_planets/transcript?language=en.

Shields, Aomawa. "The Search for Habitable Planets and Life Beyond Our Solar System." Talk. ASU Origins Project, April 5, 2016. Available online at variablestargirl.com/talks.

Singer, Philip Rodrigues. "The Art of Foley." Tutorial, Marblehead.net. Available online at www.marblehead.net/foley/index.html.

Spann, James. "How do tornadoes form?" TED-Ed, Aug. 19, 2014. Available online at www.youtube.com/watch?v=lmWh9jV_1ac.

"Tyson, Jeff. "How Animatronics Works." How Stuff Works. Available online at entertainment.howstuffworks.com/animatronic.htm.

Wall, Mike. "Hibernating Astronauts May Be Key to Mars Colonization." Space.com, Aug. 30, 2016. Available online at www.space.com/33894-mars-colonization-hibernating-astronauts-torpor.html.

Weeks, Erin. "The Science of Cotton Candy." The Raptor Lab, Oct. 21, 2013. Available online at theraptorlab.wordpress.com/2013/10/21/the-science-of-cotton-candy.

"Weird Geology: Geysers." The Museum of UnNatural Mystery. Available online at www.unmuseum.org/geysers.htm.

"What Is a Geyser?" Geology.com. Available online at geology.com/articles/geyser.shtml.

FIND OUT MORE!

Books

Chocolate: Sweet Science and Dark Secrets of the World's Favorite Treat
by Kay Frydenborg (Houghton Mifflin Harcourt, 2015)
A great read on the history and science of this treat.

Food Engineering: From Concept to Consumer
by Michael Burgan (Scholastic, 2015)
This book explores the role of science and technology in food production.

Ocean: A Visual Encyclopedia
(DK Publishing, Smithsonian, 2015)
This encyclopedia focuses on oceans and marine life.

Welcome to Mars: Making a Home on the Red Planet
by Buzz Aldrin With Marianne J. Dyson (National Geographic Kids, 2015)
Moon explorer Aldrin offers valuable insights on how humans can reach Mars and live there.

When the Earth Shakes: Earthquakes, Volcanoes, and Tsunamis *by Simon Winchester (Viking Penguin, 2015)*
Earth's most violent forces are explored in this book.

Websites

DUCKSTERS
Ducksters.com
A fun site with lots of information about science, history, geography, sports, and cool people.

GEOLOGY FOR KIDS
www.kidsgeo.com/geology-for-kids
Interesting articles about earth, rocks and landforms, cool geological formations, and more.

IT'S OK TO BE SMART
www.itsokaytobesmart.com
A fun and irreverent blog by biologist and science writer Joe Hanson

MUSEUM OF ANCIENT INVENTIONS, SMITH COLLEGE
www.smith.edu/hsc/museum/ancient_inventions/
Photographs and short articles about mind-blowing inventions of the past.

NASA
www.nasa.gov
You want information about space? The space agency has you covered. Follow the "NASA Audiences" tab to the page "for students."

NATIONAL OCEANIC AND ATMOSPHERIC ADMINISTRATION
www.noaa.gov
Tons of information about weather, climate, oceans, and much more.

Videos

CRASH COURSE KIDS
Fun videos about engineering and all sorts of science topics.
www.youtube.com/user/crashcoursekids.

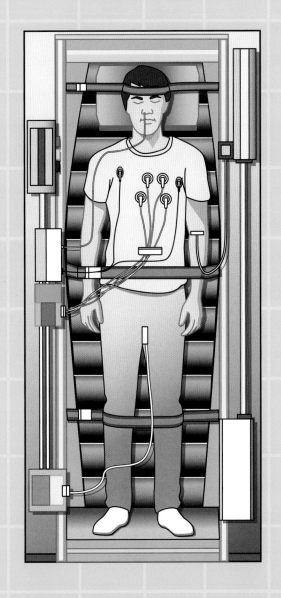

"GYROSCOPES"
Astronaut Mike Fossum demonstrates how gyroscopes are used to stabilize spacecraft in this 2013 NASA video.
www.youtube.com/watch?v=FGc5xb23XFQ.

SCISHOW KIDS
A fun look at a variety of fun and interesting science topics.
www.youtube.com/user/scishowkids.

"SHOULD WE LOOK FOR LIFE ELSEWHERE IN THE UNIVERSE?"
Astronomer and astrobiologist Aomawa Shields provides a fascinating look at the search for extraterrestrial life.
ed.ted.com/lessons/should-we-be-looking-for-life-elsewhere-in-the-universe-aomawa-shields.

INDEX

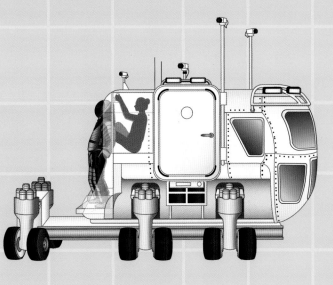

CREDITS

Dedication

For Connor, whose passion for the Earth and for knowledge always inspires me. — TJR

Acknowledgments

Special thanks to the amazing National Geographic Kids Books team—Shelby Lees, Kathryn Williams, Julide Dengel, Shannon Hibberd, Joan Gossett, the Lachina graphics team, Simon Renwick, Michelle Harris, and Roberta Lenarz—for their creativity, diligence, and support; to the Treehouse Club—Santiago Casares, David McMullin, and Shelley Walden—for their enduring friendship and critical eyes; and, as always, to Jim Monke, for understanding.

Since 1888, the National Geographic Society has funded more than 12,000 research, exploration, and preservation projects around the world. The Society receives funds from National Geographic Partners, LLC, funded in part by your purchase. A portion of the proceeds from this book supports this vital work. To learn more, visit natgeo.com/info.

For more information, visit nationalgeographic.com, call 1-800-647-5463, or write to the following address:

National Geographic Partners
1145 17th Street N.W.
Washington, D.C. 20036-4688 U.S.A.

Visit us online at nationalgeographic.com/books

For librarians and teachers: ngchildrensbooks.org

More for kids from National Geographic: natgeokids.com

National Geographic Kids magazine inspires children to explore their world with fun yet educational articles on animals, science, nature, and more. Using fresh storytelling and amazing photography, *Nat Geo Kids* shows kids ages 6 to 14 the fascinating truth about the world—and why they should care. kids.nationalgeographic.com/subscribe

For information about special discounts for bulk purchases, please contact National Geographic Books Special Sales: specialsales@natgeo.com

For rights or permissions inquiries, please contact National Geographic Books Subsidiary Rights: bookrights@natgeo.com

Library of Congress Cataloging-in-Publication Data

Names: Resler, Tamara J., author.
Title: Then and now / by T.J. Resler.
Description: Washington, DC : National Geographic Kids,[2018] | Series: How things work | Includes index. | Audience: Age: 8-12. | Audience: Grade 4 to 6.
Identifiers: LCCN 2017050026| ISBN 9781426331664 (hardcover) | ISBN 9781426331671 (hardcover)
Subjects: LCSH: Machinery--History--Juvenile literature. | Inventions--History--Juvenile literature. | Technology--History--Juvenile literature.
Classification: LCC T15 .R435 2018 | DDC 621.8--dc23
LC record available at https://lccn.loc.gov/2017050026

Printed in China
18/PPS/1